ROUTLEDGE LIBRARY EDITIONS: MILTON

Volume 5

MILTON RE-VIEWED

MILTON RE-VIEWED
Ten Essays

EDWARD LE COMTE

Routledge
Taylor & Francis Group
LONDON AND NEW YORK

First published in 1991 by Garland Publishing, Inc.

This edition first published in 2019
by Routledge
2 Park Square, Milton Park, Abingdon, Oxon OX14 4RN

and by Routledge
52 Vanderbilt Avenue, New York, NY 10017

Routledge is an imprint of the Taylor & Francis Group, an informa business

British Library Cataloguing in Publication Data
A catalogue record for this book is available from the British Library

ISBN: 978-0-367-13938-4 (Set)
ISBN: 978-0-429-20305-3 (Set) (ebk)
ISBN: 978-0-367-15143-0 (Volume 5) (hbk)
ISBN: 978-0-367-15145-4 (Volume 5) (pbk)
ISBN: 978-0-429-05533-1 (Volume 5) (ebk)

Publisher's Note
The publisher has gone to great lengths to ensure the quality of this reprint but
points out that some imperfections in the original copies may be apparent.

Disclaimer
The publisher has made every effort to trace copyright holders and would welcome
correspondence from those they have been unable to trace.

MILTON RE-VIEWED
Ten Essays

Edward Le Comte

GARLAND PUBLISHING, INC. • NEW YORK & LONDON
1991

Library of Congress Cataloging-in-Publication Data

Le Comte, Edward, 1916–
   Milton re-viewed : ten essays / Edward Le Comte.
      p.   cm. — (Garland reference library of the humanities; vol.
1446)
   ISBN 0–8153–0306–8 (acid-free paper)
   1. Milton, John, 1608–1674—Criticism and interpretation.
I. Title. II. Title: Milton reviewed. III. Series.
PR3588.L38   1991
821'.4—dc20   91–10830
                                                          CIP

Printed on acid-free, 250-year-life paper
Manufactured in the United States of America

To Peter A. Fiore, O.F.M.
editor and professor and friend:
twenty–five years of
"Venial discourse" and "Rural repast"

CONTENTS

PREFACE

These essays come in—or leave—at an unusual angle. A number of them may be unfamiliar to even a somewhat diligent researcher insofar as they appeared in places that are not the usual ones. With one exception, they were printed between 1978 and 1987. "Authorial Revision," which ends with Milton, is new, apart from the section on Milton's rendering of Horace. Some minor corrections or adjustments have been made throughout.

E. Le C.

ACKNOWLEDGMENTS

With permission, for which I am grateful, the following are here reprinted, with some updating: "Dubious Battle: Saving the Appearances,' *English Language Notes*, 19 (1982), 177–93; "Douglas Bush Remembered," *The American Scholar*, 53 (1984), 390–95; "Satan's Heresies in *Paradise Regained*," *Milton Studies*, ed., James D. Simmonds, 12 (1978; c. 1979 University of Pittsburgh Press), 253–66; "Sly Milton: The Meaning Lurking in the Contexts of His Quotations," *Greyfriar*, 19 (1978), 3–28; "Ambiguous Milton," *ibid.*, 25 (1984), 25–36; "The *Index* to the Columbia Milton: Its Virtues and Defects," *ibid.*, 28 (1987), 3–17; "Shakespeare's Emilia and Milton's: The Parameters of Research," *Milton Quarterly*, 18 (1984), 81–84; "Did Milton Mistranslate Horace?" *ibid.*, 128–29; "Miltonic Echoes in Elegia VII," *English Literary Renaissance*, 14 (1984), 191–98. The ninth essay is the Introduction (also with additions) to my edition and translation of *Justa Edovardo King*, the 1638 memorial volume in which "Lycidas" first appeared (Norwood, Pennsylvania: Norwood Editions, 1978).

Milton Re-viewed

DUBIOUS BATTLE: SAVING THE APPEARANCES

Milton's "lik'ning spiritual to corporal forms" (*PL* V. 573) alienates the modern reader. Angels fighting angels, with whatever weapons—swords, cannonballs, mountains? We no longer find war exhilarating. Nor do we believe in the materiality of angels. The heavy concentration of Latin vocabulary is also oppressive; it grides like Michael's sword. Hughes summarizes (as of 1957), "As a field marshal in Heaven, the critics agree to find Satan disgusting and to say as little as possible about him except to deplore his jibes and Belial's at the angels whom their first salvo topples over."[1] Even as a contest it is short on suspense, long on futility, since the conclusion is foregone and has already been described. Except for the hurling of hills "to and fro with jaculation dire" (VI. 685)—a scene that comes perilously close to a Superman cartoon—it is all too human. Magic might have saved it: A Midsummer Night's dream. Or it might have glided into "sci–fi":[2] ray guns, Star Wars. It does not: I do not follow Empson's charge, "unusually stupid Science Fiction."[3] In any case John Collier shunned it for his "Screenplay," even as John Dryden did for his "Opera."[4]

Dryden's omission, however, may have been due to the problem of stage presentation and the need to perfect a theory about the role of supernatural "machinery."[5] The surviving evidence is that the early readers of *Paradise Lost liked* Book VI, singled it out for praise.[6] Of the two poems that prefixed the second edition of 1674, Marvell's congratulates the author on having nothing "improper" (l. 28), while Dr. Samuel Barrow's Latin elegiacs settle on the war in Heaven as *the* most praiseworthy part. Like Marvell he finds no breach of decorum: "deceret" is his word, "Et quae Cælestes pugna deceret agros": "And fighting that befits the fields of Heaven!"[7] More than half the poem is devoted to hymning Book VI:

O, what warlike chieftains, what deeds of arms are here presented!
What dire battles here sung and with how sonorous a trumpet!

3

Celestial battle-lines and Heaven at war...! How magnificent is Lucifer, as he rises in his celestial armor, and as he strides scarce inferior to Michael himself! With what furious, with what deadly anger do they clash, while one fiercely protects the stars, the other makes them his prey! While they rend mountains and hurl them at each other as missiles and rain down fires that mortals do not know, Olympus stands doubtful to which side to yield and fears that it may not survive its own strife.

Barrow's attitude, a simple one, becomes transparent with his last lines: "Whoso shall read this poem will think that Homer sang only of frogs, Virgil only of gnats." It is not that Milton's epic is better because it is true, as Milton argued. It is better because to Milton's "grandia... Carmina" belongs the biggest subject, the biggest battle. Heaven is higher than Olympus. Michael and Christ are greater warriors than Achilles or Aeneas. The celestial warfare, by definition, dwarfs the Trojan War and the clashes of Olympians and Titans and Giants.

A bee in the bonnet, or a gnat in the ear, to which we shall ultimately have to make a response, is the belief that great poets parody themselves, that, as was still assumed in Barrow's time, not only was Virgil the author of *Culex* but *The Battle of the Frogs and Mice (Batrachomyomachia)* was Homer's own hilarious encore to *The Iliad*.

The *Essay on Translated Verse* (1684, 1685) by Wentworth Dillon, Earl of Roscommon, gives short shrift to Homer, "Whose railing heroes, and whose wounded Gods,/ Makes some suspect he snores, as well as nods."[8] But the second edition of this once famous and still praised[9] poem presents an astounding paradox. It adds twenty-seven lines of blank verse that pay Milton the sincerest compliment of imitation. With the whole wide poem before him where to choose, Roscommon picks "Raphael's numerous prose." Will it be the sublime book of Creation? No, the contemner of "wounded Gods" has no objection whatsoever to wounded angels. Far truer to Milton's content and vocabulary than style,[10] Roscommon marches right up to the cannon's mouth, then flings a few hills:

There bellowing engines, with their fiery tubes,
Dispers'd aetherial forms, and down they fell
By thousands, angels on arch-angels roll'd;
Recover'd, to the hills they ran, they flew,
Which (with their ponderous load, rocks, waters, woods)
From their firm seats torn by the shaggy tops
They bore like shields before them through the air,
Till more incens'd they hurld them at their foes.

Astonishingly, Addison referred *The Spectator* "Reader thither for some of the Master–Stroaks in the Sixth Book."[11] Newton quoted Roscommon in full.[12] Dr. Johnson's comment was, as usual, firm. Roscommon's "interposition of a long paragraph of blank verses is unwarrantably licentious."[13] It is matter for conjecture whether Johnson's annoyance was compounded in that it was Milton--and that part of Milton--that lured Roscommon away from his couplets.

Seventeenth–century critics were in agreement as to what part could not be left out in any enumeration of the highlights: "His Description of the *Pandaemonium*, his Battles of the Angels, his Creation of the World, his Digression of *Light*."[14] John Dennis wrote, "Nay, there is something so transcendently sublime in his first, second, and sixth Books."[15] Young Addison, in his "Account of the Greatest English Poets," did not ask, he stated, "How are you struck with terror and delight, / When angel with arch–angel copes in fight!"[16] The same language of being smitten, struck dumb, was used by Gildon in that same year of 1694: "you are no less astonisht at his *Description* than he makes the *Angels* to be at the Report of their Adversaries Thund'ring Fireworks."[17] Yalden was incensed at the publication of Milton's "seditious prose" in 1698, but a civil war removed to the plains of Heaven was another matter:

> Whilst here thy bold majestic numbers rise,
> And range th'embattled legions of the skies,
> With armies fill the azure plains of light,
> And paint the lively terrors of the fight,
> We own the poet worthy to rehearse
> Heaven's lasting triumphs in immortal verse;
> But when thy impious mercenary pen
> Insults the best of princes, best of men,
> Our admiration turns to just disdain,
> And we revoke the fond applause again.[18]

Meanwhile in 1695 the London schoolmaster Patrick Hume,[19] who knew Greek and Latin and Hebrew, provided for less learned readers the first notes to *Paradise Lost*, the prime source, directly or indirectly, for editors and annotators ever since. (For instance, Arthur O. Lovejoy traced "felix culpa" quotation back to J. Richardson, but Richardson borrowed his learning--from Hume.[20]) Besides establishing Milton's precedents in Book VI, Hume distributed some compliments (and absolutely no objections) among his notes, such as "probable" (l. 368), "A noble Description" (l. 511), "this noble Description" (l. 751), or "A Wonderful Description of the Dreadful and Destructive *Terrestrial Thunder*" (l. 586). Dryden had elevated Milton above Homer and Virgil in his "Epigram" for the fourth edition of *Paradise Lost*. In this sixth edition Hume quotes at

VI. 209 the *Iliad* and the *Aeneid*, then asserts, "Neither of 'em does so fully set forth *the Scene of Horrour*." But the English poet also surpasses his rivals in conciseness, e.g., Homer is "Much more loose and redundant than our *Expressive Author*" (l. 339). As for Tasso, he "has employed a whole Stanza to express the same, less significantly" (l. 406). The cannon are a just inclusion (l. 504). Nothing could be more admirable than the "jaculation dire" (l. 665).

In his 1698 "The Life of John Milton," which was the longest, if not the fullest, to date, John Toland inserted as virtually the only commentary Barrow's Latin poem,[21] thus completing a remarkable circle of unanimous praise for that which makes us wince, or (Waldock's word) giggle.[22] The only demurral came from two theological writers, who had a battle–axe to grind.

First there was the versatile Sir Samuel Morland (himself lately gone blind), who in *The Urim of Conscience* (1695) declares he will not,

> in imitation of a late very learned Author, try to squeeze a plausible Description of *Lost Paradise* out of *St. John's* Vision in the isle of *Patmos*, and fancy to myself a formal and pitcht Battle, upon a vast and wide Plain, in the North part of Heaven, fought between two mighty Hosts of Blessed and Revolted Spirits, conducted and led up by mighty Arch–Angels (for their Generals) riding in Brazen Chariots, drawn by foaming Steeds and clad with *Adamantine* Coats, one of which was, by a massy Sword, cut down to the wast, and stained with Angelic blood. Where the one of these Armies dug up the Terrain of Heaven, and with the Materials they there found, made Powder, Bullets, and great Guns (it is a pity that Bombs were not in use when he wrote that Treatise) and with them did great execution upon their Enemies, who in revenge tore up great Mountains by the Roots, and hurl'd them at their Heads, with a great number of other Romantic Stories, which is to jest with God's word, and much fitter for Poets and Painters, who when they are got to the top of Parnassus, frame to themselves Idea's of what Chimera's or Goblins they please.[23]

In Robert H. West's words, "Morland is disturbed that the imaginative success of Milton's scene may pass it with some for doctrine."[24]

Charles Leslie made the same point in 1698 in *The History of Sin and Heresy*:

> The gravity and seriousness with which this subject ought to be treated, has not been regarded in the adventrous flight of Poets, who have dress'd Angels in Armour, and put Swords and Guns into their Hands, to form romantick Battels in the Plains of Heaven, a

scene of licentious fancy; but the Truth has been greatly hurt thereby....[25]

Morland and Leslie were not making literary objections but objecting to literature that enlarges upon Holy Writ to the detriment of faith and truth. They are reminiscent of Calvin's admonition against "inane fable" and the "dwell[ing] upon unprofitable subjects."[26] For both Morland and Leslie "romantic(k)" is a bad word. Milton's self-admitted early attraction to "lofty Fables and Romances"[27] led to forbidden fruit. The two critics in their polemic zeal come close to mockery, a note that others will strike for other reasons. We are on the way to, for instance, Pococurante, who derives no pleasure from his first edition because, for one thing, Milton was led astray by a romance: he "imitates seriously Ariosto's comical invention of firearms by making the devils fire a cannon in Heaven."[28]

Where Pococurante, "little caring," the jaded lord, was disgusted with a borrowing from *Orlando Furioso*, where Leslie and Morland found it a poet's duty "not to expatiate into effeminate romance, but to express Truth,"[29] Addison was to teach that the pleasure in Book VI consisted in recognizing Milton's sources, enjoying his virtuoso echoes. If you know where the battle came from, you cannot fail to appreciate it.

> The second Day's Engagement is apt to startle an Imagination, which has not been raised and qualified for such a Description, by the Reading of the ancient Poets, and of *Homer* in particular....Such Engines were the only Instruments [Lucifer] could have made use of to imitate those Thunders, that in all Poetry, both Sacred and Prophane, are represented as the Arms of the Almighty. The Tearing up the Hills was not altogether so daring a Thought as the former. We are, in some measure, prepared for such an Incident by the Description of the Gyants' War, which we meet with among the ancient Poets.

The English poet has outdone the ancients, whose "Ideas" sometimes "savour more of Burlesque than of the Sublime." The plucking of "the seated Hills" passage is in perfect taste: "We have the full Majesty of *Homer* in this short Description, improved by the Imagination of *Claudian*, without its Puerilities." Michael's sword "from the armoury of God" has admirable precedents in Virgil, Homer, the Book of Maccabees. Moloch in bellowing retreat is Mars (Ares) in the *Iliad*, but "*Milton* has kept all the Horrour of this Image without running into the Ridicule of it." "Horrour" rivals "Sublime" as a word of praise. "As *Homer* has introduced into his Battel of the Gods every thing that is great and terrible in Nature, *Milton* has filled his Fight of Good and Bad Angels with all the like

Circumstances of Horrour." One must marvel what genius can do, "strengthened by all the Helps of Learning."

"The helps of learning": thence runs an ongoing apology for Book VI continuous from the first editor to the latest articles and editions and books. The more precedents Milton had the more justified he is. Building upon Watson Kirkconnell's massive catalogue and anthology of analogues, taking advantage of modern hexaemeral studies, Stella Revard produced (after twenty years) *The War in Heaven: "Paradise Lost" and the Tradition of Satan's Rebellion,* which reviews Daemonomachiae or Angeleida in Renaissance authors who range alphabetically from Acevedo, Agnifilo, Alexander, Alfano, Andreini, to Valmarana, Valvasone, Vida, and Vondel. Roland M. Frye has called attention to the paintings that Milton might have seen or that establish the iconographic tradition. Michael or Christ in armor with sword and shield was often depicted downing the devil. In the 1522 Wittenberg Bible "Cranach illustrated the rebel angels as knights clad in full plate armor."[30] Jacques Callot drew demonic cannon. If you have gazed upon certain works by Luca Giordano, Spinello Aretino, Peter Bruegel the Elder, Tintoretto, Rubens, Piero della Francesca, Jimenez, Antonio Pollaiuolo, Lotto, Guido Reni, Domenico Beccafumi, little in Book VI will surprise you, not even the "fiery steeds" (ll. 17, 391) (about which it is useless to ask what they are doing in Heaven and whether they are immortal). Dr. Johnson asserted, "no precedents can justify absurdity," but Frye answers, "what is or is not regarded as absurd is often governed by precedent."[31]

Addison's calculably influential Saturday essays provided, then, an apology that has endured to the present, even as each reprint of them boosted the epic's fame. But in that year of 1712 Alexander Pope was finishing the most devastating comment ever made on VI. Addison (himself the author of a Latin poem on the battle of the pygmies and cranes) in recommending that Pope not expand *The Rape of the Lock* could not have foreseen the deflating effect of--let us limit it--one couplet. Milton (as Pope himself quoted) wrote of Satan's impermanent wound by Michael's "griding sword": "but th' Ethereal substance clos'd / Not long divisible" (330-331). Pope wrote of the Baron's two-fingered engine, "Fate urged the shears, and cut the Sylph in twain / (But airy substance soon unites again)" (III. 151-152). That was a snip heard round the critical world.

Things will never be the same again. As Voltaire said, "Methinks the true Criterion for discerning what is really ridiculous in an *Epick Poem,* is to examine if the same Thing would not fit exactly the Mock Heroick."[32] Voltaire eventually practiced what he preached by incorporating Milton's angelic battles into his burlesque epic *La Pucelle* (1755).[33] To come down to the mid-1970's, a note in Pope's *Iliad* (II. 255) about "ludicrous descriptions" prompts Barbara Lewalski to mention "the mock–epic features (bathos, ludicrous situations, outrageous puns) of the War in Heaven."[34]

True, eighteenth–century praise of VI streams forth, particularly among the versifiers,[35] both before and after Addison. Even "slashing Bentley" struck a reverential note at verse 212: "Now our Author is come to that Part of his Poem, where he is most to exert what Faculty he has of *hupsos:* Magniloquence of Stile, and Sublimity of Thought."[36] The nonsense Bentley found and emended consisted of an occasional ill– chosen word: not "*Nectarous* humor" (l. 332) from the wounds (it is not a drink), but "*Ichorous.*" Change "*Cubic* Phalanx" (l. 399) to "*Martial*": "To make it *Cubic*, it must be as high, as it's broad." Jonathan Richardson, two years later, possessing a painter's eye, interrupted his expository notes to rhapsodize: "Here will be seen a Battle–Picture, Such as No Pen Before, nor any Pencil has shown to the World. *Homer's* are Not Such...What follows in the Second Days War is more Amazingly Sublime than the Sublimity of the First."[37] Newton, deploying Addison's word, "horror," also notes a fine progression: "It is remark'd by the critics in praise of Homer's battels, that they rise in horror one above another...The same may be said of Milton's battels" (note at l. 669).

But as *Paradise Lost* became a monument it would inevitably be pelted; the more readers it had the greater the likelihood that some would discover defects among the "beauties." Did not Pope himself, who yielded to none in loving imitation, complain: "In quibbles Angel and Archangel join, / And God the Father turns a School–divine" ("First Epistle of the Second Book of Horace," ll. 101–102). Voltaire praised much in his *Epick Poetry* essay, but, a few paragraphs after suggesting mock–heroic applicability of the "ridiculous," he assaulted VI at length, using the same word: "the very Thing which is so dreadfully great on Earth, becomes very low and ridiculous in Heaven."[38] "Ridiculous" also became John Clarke's adjective: "it looks ridiculous at first Sight, to represent them as cutting, slashing, and stabbing one another." Clarke added "ludicrous" for good measure: Milton "has, with great Imprudence and Irreverence, engaged the Son of God in such a ludicrous Piece of Fiction."[39] Lyttleton found "the *poetica licentia* is stretched too far, and *the just* is sacrificed to *the wonderful.*"[40] Dennis, in a different context, precisely anticipated Johnson's objection: "the Poet seems to confound Body and Mind, Spirit and Matter."[41]

Johnson, then, was definitive rather than new when, sixty–five years after the publication of *The Rape of the Lock*, he phrased his famous stricture: "The confusion of spirit and matter, which pervades the whole narration of the war in heaven, fills it with incongruity; and the book in which it is related is, I believe, the favourite of children, and gradually neglected, as knowledge is increased."[42]

Knowledge did increase. With the increase have come various defenses besides that already mentioned of poetical and pictorial precedent. For instance, there is the matter (so to speak) of pneumatology. Perhaps Milton knew more about angels than Dr. Johnson did. Clarke was wrong in designating angels "Immaterial Beings."[43] That expert theologian, C.S. Lewis, found that "Milton's picture of the angels, though doubtless poetical in detail, is meant in principle as a literally true picture of what they probably were according to the up-to-date pneumatology of his century."[44] Those out of touch with Wierus, Psellus, Bodin, can read Burton, whom Lewis, before going on to Henry More,[45] quotes quoting Psellus. Devils, at least, "are nourished and have excrements,...feel pain if they be hurt."[46] The author of *The Anatomy*, presciently smiling at poems yet unwritten, adds, "if their bodies be cut, with admirable celerity they come together again." The angelology briefly sketched by Lewis gets expanded in West's far-ranging *Milton and the Angels*. There is a tradition of solidity that dates as far back as to Tertullian, if not the Bible.[47]

Another explanation has to do with "accommodation": "what surmounts the reach / Of human sense, I shall delineate so, / By lik'ning spiritual to corporal forms, / As may express them best" (V. 571-574). "What surmounts the reach / Of human sense" becomes "things above us" in Dryden's preface to *The State of Innocence, and the Fall of Man*:

> For Immaterial Substances we are authoriz'd by Scripture in their description: and herein the Text accommodates it self to vulgar apprehension, in giving Angels the likeness of beautiful young men. Thus, after the Pagan Divinity, has *Homer* drawn his Gods with humane Faces: and thus we have notions of things above us, by describing them like other beings more within our knowledge.[48]

The theory of accommodation had its stamen in Hebrews 9.23-24 and flourished in Augustine and Aquinas and the Renaissance. Its branches include Neoplatonism and typology.[49] Who can deny an apology given by the "divine / Historian" (VIII. 6-7)--or shall we now say mythologist-- himself?

Well, Raphael can deny it, for he proceeds to undercut what he has just said: "though what if Earth / Be but the shadow of Heav'n, and things therein / Each to other like, more than on Earth is thought?" (V. 574-576). This is one of those places where, as with the Ptolemaic and Copernican theories, Milton has his cake and eats it too. We are led to consider the possibility that the surface and *significatio* of VI are the same, that Milton, though "Not sedulous by Nature to indite / Wars, hitherto the only Argument / Heroic deem'd" (IX. 27-29), did what he had to do with a flourish. As even the caustic Waldock admits, "The war had to be described."[50] It is Revelation (12.7) that "there was war in Heaven." "War cannot be made without weapons; and Milton's only fault is that he has rather exaggerated than minimized the difficulties": so Garnett in 1890.[51] Waldock complains of inconsistent alternation of matter and spirit.[52] But it is characteristic of this most competitive, and most inclusive, of poets both to have the Aonian mount and soar above it, to draw on Homer and to out-Homer Homer. It would be, not a war to end all wars (though it would be one to begin them), but a description to end- -by surpassing--all war descriptions. He studied military manuals[53] as well as the poets and historians. Are we prepared to assert that all those early readers who were roused, charmed, and smitten were oafs, or "children," totally lacking in literary sensibility?

Arnold Stein would call such readers (if he mentioned them) naive. He says of the "So Hills amid the Air encounter'd Hills" passage (VI. 664–668): "Surely it is naive to think Milton straining for grandeur in this passage."[54] Book VI is not to be taken literally at all. It is extended metaphor, comic in intention and in effect. Where John Peter will complain of "the Disney-like panoramas,"[55] Stein, reaching further back in film history, is reminded of the throwing of custard pies--and relishes it. Or, on a more dignified level: "The dominant mood of the war is like nothing so much as a scherzo, a kind of great scherzo, like some of Beethoven's--with more than human laughter, too elevated, and comprehensive, and reverberating not to be terribly funny" (p. 20). Stein points to the numerous instances of ridicule. It is the literary critic--not the scholars, with their helps of learning--to whom it is left to penetrate the symbolism, to understand, for instance, that "The invention of artillery is an attempt to usurp ultimate moral might by means of matter" (p. 37). Peter, naming Stein, will murmur against those apologists for *Paradise Lost* who "praise its faults, but darkly, as occult successes" (p. 159), but the fact remains that Stein's interpretation, ever since it first appeared as an article in 1951, has met with wide approval. It is enshrined in the latest edition of Hanford's *Handbook* and in two collections of essays.[56] Hanford's successor as the "dean" of Miltonists, Douglas Bush, labels it "persuasive."[57] Most helpfully, it turns an embarrassment into a triumph. The great modern literary virtue is irony, and now Milton turns out to have it, along with a sense of humor previously denied. In the words of Stanley Fish, one of Stein's converts, "Miltonic humour is never side- splitting, but [now] there is more than a smile."[58]

However, there are problems, one could say serious problems. Recalling the poet's aim, to justify the ways of God to men, we must be careful whom and what we laugh at. Milton is not Anatole France, whose 1914 novel *La Révolte des Anges* imitates VI so closely (chs. xviii and xxxv) for purposes of light and unmistakable irony. That there is much derision in VI does not mean that all is mocked. "Be not deceived: God is not mocked" (Galatians 6.7). Stein has tarred--or tickled--all the personages with the same brush, indiscriminately. In an implicit criticism of Stein, Joseph H. Summers distinguishes points of view: "From the divine point of view the entire devilish attempt is comic and absurd; from the point of view of the unfallen angels the action is truly heroic; from that of Satan and his crew it is ultimately tragic--the calamitous fall of princes from great place. The reader is invited to share all of these points of view at various moments."[59]

Alastair Fowler finds "burlesque...most unlikely in view of the undoubtedly serious concluding phase, Messiah's victory"[60] (which even Peter, 80, concedes is a "stirring climax"). Murray Roston in *Milton and the Baroque* employs both textual analysis and art history to refute Stein. We must not "impose a modernistic reading on the text," which will "emasculate its imaginative force" when we are fortunate to possess "a solemnly conceived scene of immense vigour and turmoil, a baroque clash of forces such as Rubens would have delighted to paint."[61] Roston returns us to the helps of learning, the wrong "modern response" being "due to the lapse in time since the period of its composition, and a change of viewpoint which a knowledge of his era and his specifically baroque aims may help to dispel" (p. 121). Where Fowler declares the war "is fought solely to amplify the transcendence of Christ" (note to 122–123), Roston views the ending as a typically "baroque demonstration of divine might" (p. 129).

Stein was the stimulus for others (he inspired Revard's comprehensive book) to search for--and discover--meaning in an otherwise unsatisfactory episode. While Marjorie Nicolson continued to see "largely straightforward narration, involving almost no philosophical or theological problems,"[62] Priscilla St. George found "Psychomachia in Books V and VI,"[63] a battle of souls which would be more plausible if *Paradise Lost* were *The Faerie Queene*. (In "An Hymne of Heavenly Love," ll. 78–91, one "breath" of the Almighty blows his opponents to Hell.) Fish drew the lesson of "the true (inner) heroism of obedience" (p. 197), even in the most useless and therefore the most trying of circumstances. Northrop Frye said, "the symbolism of the three–day war in heaven is designed to show that the total angelic power of action is contained in the Son of God."[64] Is there reference to the Crucifixion, the Resurrection, and the Last Judgment?[65] The numerologists have a field day.[66] (VI is the center, but does the center hold?) What about "an eschatological interpretation of the overwhelming of Pharaoh's forces and the redemption of the Children of Israel"?[67] Or "a celestial archetype of the future warfare between the church and its enemies"?[68] This is Steadman; Christopher Hill infers topical allusions to the Civil War, the first battle being, for example, "as inconclusive as Edgehill."[69] For Donald F. Bouchard there is a more sinister point, of the levelling effect of violence.[70] Helen Gardner sees "a parable of the war of good and evil as long as the world lasts, a struggle in which good, though tested to the uttermost, cannot be overcome, but also cannot overcome."[71]

Like Hanford and Wright before her, and Wilding and Revard after her, Dame Helen also finds a statement against war, or the futility of war.[72] This is convincing and certainly popular for our time, provided we are not led to the extreme of calling Milton a pacifist, which he was not. A 1980 book goes astray by assuming—but not demonstrating—"Milton's Disapproval of War."[73] The best surveyor of this subject, Ruth Mohl, after starting out with "surely" (a word regularly used for the conjectural and the wishful)—"Surely no one ever detested war more than did Milton"— proceeds to quote in the next page the uncompromising statement in *Christian Doctrine* (ll. 17): "There seems no reason why war should be unlawful now, any more than in the time of the Jews; nor is it anywhere forbidden in the New Testament."[74] Appropriate here are the impressions of that sensitive critic G. Wilson Knight, who in 1939 (three years before he found that Milton had prophesied Hitler) remarked, "Anything metallic takes his eye; his is a polished, burnished, almost a brazen universe."[75] We may hate the "spit and polish" of military formation (it bored Taine a century ago[76]), but Milton displayed great interest in it from Book I, even as at eighteen he was doing a Gunpowder Plot epyllion that bears detailed resemblance to his epic.[77] Knight further noted: "the poem is built expressly of brazen clangours and dulcet harmonies" (p. 56). Book VI is an indispensable part of these contrasts and alternations: indeed music itself, including heavenly music, comes from metal as well as voice, the harps and the trumpets.

I am fascinated by a passing comment of Broadbent's that we have a case of self-parody. (None of these critics raises the question of "the intentional fallacy.") Broadbent gives an explanation why the eighteenth century was drawn to VI: "In the Peace of the Augustans it must have appeared an enviable first-hand exercise in Homerics, not original but at least paraphrastic, when all they could manage was translation" (p. 218). But Milton (I infer) had some well-founded doubts of his own success and therefore from the vantage point of his great Book IX issued an apology, "Not sedulous...to indite / Wars," etc. Raphael had perhaps already reflected the author's own uneasiness: "strange to us it seem'd / At first, that Angel should with Angel war, / And in fierce hosting meet" (VI. 91–93). Matthew Arnold declared (what the translator he was criticizing, Francis Newman, denied), "Homer is plain in his words and style."[78] Virgil is less plain. Milton is still less plain, because he felt imitation in English would have to proffer Greek or Latin locutions. His worst style is a corruption of his best. He will commit (as Fowler annotates), "bomphiologia (excessively lofty diction)": "thir Balls / Of missive ruin; part incentive reed / Provide, pernicious with one touch to fire" (VI. 513– 520). Or he will plummet to "diction that is indecorously low": "Embowell'd with outrageous noise the Air, / And all her entrails tore, disgorging foul/ Thir devilish glut" (VI. 587–589).[79] Both passages lead straight to *The Splendid Shilling*: "from Tube as black / As Winter- Chimney, or well-polish'd Jet, / Exhale *Mundungus*, ill-perfuming Scent: / Not blacker Tube, nor of a shorter Size / Smoaks *Cambro–Britain*."[80]

All this in VI can be found to have a moral point, because applied to the forces of evil. So can their bad puns. Maybe indeed the message is that language degenerates with morals: the fallen angels are getting worse with every utterance as with every action.[81]

We still have the problem that the good are not differentiated from the bad. Raphael puns too.[82] Even the great onrush of "The Chariot of Paternal Deity" (l. 750), with its biblical echoes, is contaminated by pagan reminiscences that have the appearance of uncontrolled learning rather than irony, since we cannot--at least I cannot--suppose Milton would be ironical about Christ. "Nor longer then did Jove / Curb down his force; but sudden in his soul / There grew dilated strength, and it was filled / With his omnipotence: his whole of might / Broke from him, and the godhead rushed abroad. / The vaulted sky--" This is Hesiod.[83] Progressive revelation? Ancient myths as foreshadowing Christian truths? But we are directed not only to the chief Olympian but to a mere mortal, Hector, one who preserved the citadel no better than the good angels did. The signal is, "Gloomy as Night" (l. 832), which is *Iliad* XII. 463. Newton noted this, but no commentator gives the next parallel: Hector's lashed horses "carried the running chariot among Achaians and Trojans, / trampling down dead men and shields" (*Iliad* XI. 533-534): the clear precursor of "O'er Shield and Helms, and helmed heads he rode / Of Thrones and mighty Seraphim prostrate" (ll. 840-841).[84] The only differences are that the Son of God's chariot is self-propelled--Knight calls it "a super-tank"[85]--and that the All-Conqueror, in a grim parody of salvation, lifts up the bodies he has ridden over ("The overthrown he rais'd," l. 856) in order to run them out of Heaven.

In my view, which is skeptical of the epicycles and orbs of modern criticism, Milton, being a materialist, whose angels digest and blush and make love--as well as bleed--aimed for solidity on the heavenly battlefield too. He had little taste for symbolism, denying it even to the Song of Solomon (IX. 442) and not giving it to Revelation 12. 7-9 in *De Doctrina Christiana* (1.9). His style veered out of control at times, and he did not always keep his inner eye on details, as Wayne Shumaker and others have pointed out.[86] After spending some years gathering upwards of 1,600 verbal ambiguities in Milton's poetry, I came to the conclusion that "ambivalence" is "a major characteristic of Milton's mind and style."[87] Others have reached the same conclusion on different grounds.[88] Back in 1945 C.M. Bowra was saying:

> His epic precedents demanded more of Milton than incidental decoration, and especially they demanded scenes of battle. Milton must have been in two minds about this. He felt strongly that military prowess was no real heroism, and no doubt after the Restoration, if not earlier, he was thoroughly disillusioned of any hopes that an army could reform society. At the same time, both as

a scholar and as a man, he had known the excitement and the glamour of war and felt a genuine admiration for generals of the Commonwealth. His interest in war shows itself even when he speaks in disapproval, as in his account of Cain's descendants with its Homeric battle–scenes: "On each hand slaughter and gigantic deeds." (XI. 659) To solve this discord in himself he had to find a war which really contented his conscience and into which he could put more than the old heroic fury.[89]

But he also put in that "old heroic fury." The resulting parody is not of that pointed sort that gave us, for instance, The Unholy Trinity.[90] The great virtuoso has fallen into habit and struck a few false notes, as far as modern taste goes. "He himself may sometimes be tired, and simply kept going by the habit of the grand manner."[91] Looking back he himself worried about "tedious havoc" (IX. 30). If one may be allowed to repeat, for the sake of expanding, a cliché, Milton wanted to have his cake and eat it too, but the assimilation was not quite of the angelic quality. It does not help a fairly plain––or overfancy––situation to beg the question as Edwin Greenlaw, that pioneer of modern revisionism, did in a different context seventy–four years ago: "The story...immediately gains significance and interest if we recognize...a symbol, and that Milton's real theme is––."[92] To steal a word from two other debaters, "Doubtless!" (I. 315; IX. 745).

NOTES

1. Merritt Y. Hughes, ed., Milton's *Complete Poems and Major Prose*
    (New York: Odyssey Press, 1957), 178. I quote *Paradise Lost* from
    this edition. Hughes's 1958 article, "Milton's Celestial Battle and
    the Theogonies," reprinted in his *Ten Perspectives on Milton* (New
    Haven: Yale University Press, 1965), 196–219, reviews some
    criticism of the 1940's and the 1950's that I do not repeat. Stella
    Purce Revard classifies much recent criticism in bibliographical
    footnotes, especially on 18–26, in *The War in Heaven: "Paradise
    Lost" and the Tradition of Satan's Rebellion* (Ithaca: Cornell
    University Press, 1980). See also "Milton's Visual Imagination and
    the Critics" and "The War in Heaven and the Expulsion of the
    Rebel Angels," 8–19, 43 ff. of *Milton's Imagery and the Visual
    Arts: Iconographic Tradition in the Epic Poems* by Roland M. Frye
    (Princeton: Princeton University Press, 1978). Charles Martindale
    uses the word "surrealism." *John Milton and the Transformation of
    Ancient Epic* (Totowa, N.J.: Barnes & Noble Books, 1986),
    219.Tennyson, as might be expected, preferred the pastoral part.
    "Me rather all that bowery loneliness, / The brooks of Eden," etc.
    "Milton," *Works* (New York: Macmillan, 1913), 237. But 19th–
    century oratorio composers made music of it, beginning with Sir
    Henry Rowley Bishop's *The Battle of the Angels* (London, 1820)
    and continuing with Anton Rubinstein and Theodore Du Bois. See
    Revard, "From the State of Innocence to the Fall of Man: The
    Fortunes of *Paradise Lost* as Opera and Oratorio," in *Milton's
    Legacy in the Arts*, ed., Albert C. Labriola and Edward Sichi, Jr.
    (University Park: Pennsylvania State University Press, 1988), 116
    ff.
2. Cf. J.B. Broadbent, *Some Graver Subject* (London: Chatto &
    Windus, 1960), 223. Harry Blamires finds modern science in the
    angelic corporeal flexibility: "interesting analogies very much in
    line with what we are now in the post–relativity era learning about
    the limitations of our own scales of observation, modes of
    awareness, and dimensional constrictedness." *Milton's Creation*
    (London: Methuen, 1971), 155–156.
3. William Empson, *Milton's God* (Norfolk, Conn.: New Directions,
    1961), 54.
4. Collier, *Milton's "Paradise Lost": Screenplay for Cinema of the
    Mind* (New York: Knopf, 1973); Dryden, *The State of Innocence,
    and the Fall of Man* (London, 1677).
5. On the latter see George Williamson, *Milton and Others* (Chicago:
    University of Chicago Press, 1965), 109 ff.
6. Thus it sweeps too far back in time to speak of "the dissatisfaction
    with Books V and VI which many readers have expressed from the

seventeenth century until today." Joseph H. Summers, "The Embarrassments of *Paradise Lost*," 69 in *Approaches to "Paradise Lost,"* ed., C.A. Patrides (London: Edward Arnold, 1968). Nor is there any warrant for lumping Addison with Johnson in disapproval, as William G. Riggs does (*The Christian Poet in "Paradise Lost"* [Berkeley: University of California Press, 1972]. 115). Addison disapproved only of the puns. See Edward Le Comte, *A Dictionary of Puns in Milton's English Poetry* (New York: Columbia University Press, 1981), vii–viii. Edward W. Tayler calls them "lousy.' *Milton's Poetry: Its Development in Time* (Pittsburgh: Duquesne University Press, 1979), 97.

7. Barrow's lines are regularly dropped from editions and even the Columbia *Works* does not print a translation. I quote Nelson G. McCrea's in *The Student's Milton*, ed., Frank A. Patterson, 2d ed., (New York: Crofts, 1933), Notes on Poetry, 69–70. Interestingly enough, the only occurrence of "indecent" in Milton's poetry is at VI. 601.

8. *Works of the English Poets* (London, 1779), X, 218.

9. *The Oxford History of English Literature* praises it more than the *Cambridge History of English Literature* (Charles Whibley in the latter, VIII, 250–252); James Sutherland, *English Literature of the Late Seventeenth Century* (Oxford: Oxford University Press, 1969), 170.

10. See Raymond D. Havens, *The Influence of Milton on English Poetry* (Cambridge, Mass.: Harvard University Press, 1922), 89.

11. *The Spectator*, No. 333, 22 March 1712, III, 48, in Everyman's Library, ed., G. Gregory Smith (London: Dent, 1907). All my quotations, below, from this Addison essay are in the compass of 46–51.

12. Thomas Newton, ed., *Paradise Lost* (Dublin, 1773), I, 499–500.

13. Life of Roscommon in Johnson's *Works* (Oxford:Talboys and Wheeler, 1825), VII, 171.

14. *Athenian Mercury*, 16 January 1692, in *Milton: The Critical Heritage*, ed., John T. Shawcross (London: Routledge & Kegan Paul, 1970), 98.

15. "The Preface to *The Passion of Byblis*" (1692), in Shawcross, 99.

16. Shawcross, 105.

17. "Vindication of *Paradise Lost*," attributed to Charles Gilden, in Shawcross, 108.

18. Thomas Yalden, "On the Reprinting of Milton's Prose Works," Shawcross, 122.

19. *Annotations on Milton's "Paradise Lost."* In a curious note to X. 1003, "Why stand we longer shivering under fears," Hume shows his ambiance: "A Metaphor from Boys quaking and shaking as they enter the cold Stream by degrees, but cured by plunging in."

20. Lovejoy, "Milton and the Paradox of the Fortunate Fall" (1937), in *Critical Essays on Milton from "ELH"* (Baltimore: Johns Hopkins University Press, 1969), 171. Lovejoy did not discover Hume's note because it is not where one would expect to find it, applied to XII. 473 ff., but occurs instead at III. 342.

21. Helen Darbishire, ed., *The Early Lives of Milton* (London: Constable, 1932), 184–185.

22. A.J.A. Waldock, *"Paradise Lost" and its Critics* (Cambridge: Cambridge University Press, 1947), 112.

23. 13–14, as quoted by Robert H. West, *Milton and the Angels* (Athens, Ga.: University of Georgia Press, 1955), 118. I believe Richard Garnett was the first to call attention to *The Urim of Conscience. Life of John Milton* (London: W. Scott, [1890]), 163.

24. West, 118.

25. Shawcross, 117.

26. Calvin, quoted (not in this context) by Revard, 69; see also 109, 132. The principal locus is Bk. I, ch. 14 of the *Institutes*.

27. *An Apology* in *Works* (New York: Columbia University Press, 1931), III, 304.

28. Voltaire, *Candide*, ch. xxv (New York: Modern Library, n.d.), 124.

29. Leslie in Shawcross, 118.

30. Frye, 46.

31. Johnson, VII, 137; Frye, 44, n. 5.

32. Shawcross, 253.

33. See Jean Gillet, *"Le Paradis Perdu" dans la Littérature Française de Voltaire à Chateaubriand* (Paris: Librarie Klincksieck, 1975), 84.

34. "On looking into Pope's Milton," *EA*, 27 (1974), 499; *Milton S*, 11 (1978), 46.

35. See poems numbered 31, 37, 38, 46, 79, 139, 163, 171, 178, 203 in John Walter Good, *Studies in the Milton Tradition* (Urbana: University of Illinois Press, 1915), 61–107.

36. Ed., *Milton's "Paradise Lost"* (London, 1732). I transliterate the Greek word.

37. *Explanatory Notes and Remarks on Milton's "Paradise Lost"* (London, 1734), 258–259.

38. Shawcross, 256.

39. Shawcross, 262, 264.

40. Shawcross, 257.

41. Shawcross, 240.

42. VII, 136–137.

43. Shawcross, 262.

44. *A Preface to "Paradise Lost"* (London: Oxford University Press, 1942), 105.

45. Whom Marjorie H. Nicolson discovered: "The Spirit World of Milton and More," *SP*, 22 (1925), 433–452. In fact Henry John Todd quoted Burton in 1801. Ed., *Poetical Works* (London), note to VI. 344.

46. Robert Burton, *The Anatomy of Melancholy*, "A Digression of the Nature of Spirits," Everyman's Library, I, 182. Frye is wrong to say (and gracefully acknowledged his mistake when I pointed it out) that Milton's good angels "feel pain" (54). They are "unobnoxious to be pain'd" (VI. 404), while the rebels are "now gross by sinning grown" (661).

47. For bibliographical updating see C.A. Patrides, *Milton and the Christian Tradition* (Oxford: Oxford University Press, 1966), 46–48.

48. In Edward W. Tayler, ed., *Literary Criticism of Seventeenth–Century England* (New York: Knopf, 1967), 341.

49. William G. Madsen sorts these distinctions out in *From Shadowy Types to Truth: Studies in Milton's Symbolism* (New Haven: Yale University Press, 1968).

50. 109.

51. 163.

52. 109–111.

53. James H. Hanford, "Milton and the Art of War" (1921), reprinted in *John Milton, Poet and Humanist* (Cleveland: Western Reserve University Press, 1966), 185–223; James A. Freeman, *Milton and the Martial Muse* (Princeton: Princeton University Press, 1980).

54. *Answerable Style: Essays on "Paradise Lost"* (Minneapolis: University of Minnesota Press, 1953), 24. This section first appeared as an article, "Milton's War in Heaven--An extended Metaphor," *ELH*, 18 (1951), 201–220. A contributor to *Gentleman's Magazine* for March, 1738 anticipated Stein by 213 years: "that foolish Apparatus of the apostate Spirits, their Cannon and Balls, and Powder and Matches, all described in such a Manner, and with such a Train of ludicrous Circumstances, as would make one believe he intended a Joke by it?" In Shawcross, *Milton 1732–1801: The Critical Heritage* (London: Routledge & Kegan Paul, 1972), 95. In his latest book Louis L. Martz well sums up the critical problem: "is the writing simply awkward and inflated and unsure, or is it a deliberate creation of heroic parody?" Influenced by recent reinterpretations of Ovid's *Metamorphoses*, Martz opts for the latter (*Poet of Exile: A Study of Milton's Poetry* [New Haven: Yale University Press, 1980], 210).

55. *A Critique of "Paradise Lost"* (New York: Columbia University Press, 1960), 77.

56. Hanford and James G. Taaffe, *A Milton Handbook*, 5th ed. (New York: Meredith, 1970), 173–174; Arthur E. Barker, ed., *Milton: Modern Essays in Criticism* (New York: Oxford University Press, 1965), 264–283; Martz, ed., *Milton: A Collection of Critical Essays* (Englewood Cliffs, N.J.: Prentice Hall, 1966), 148–155.

57. In *A Milton Encyclopedia*, ed., William B. Hunter, Jr. et al. (Lewisburg: Bucknell University Press, 1979), VI, 69. In *John Milton* (New York: Macmillan, 1964), Bush found "the range of significance... wide, from the immediate rendering of Satan's anarchic passion and violence (which is a lesson for Adam) to the monstrous confusion and waste of human wars and perhaps a typological foreshadowing of Armageddon and the second coming of Christ" (157).

58. *Surprised by Sin* (New York: St. Martin's Press, 1967), 173.

59. *The Muse's Method* (Cambridge: Harvard University Press, 1962), 122.

60. *Poems*, ed., John Carey and Alastair Fowler (London: Longmans, 1968). Twenty years later Margarita Stocker was to call Stein's "an apparently illogical suggestion, since it is unlikely that Milton would wish to ridicule the loyal angels at any rate." *Paradise Lost* (Atlantic Highlands, N.J.: Humanities Press International, 1988), 31.

61. (London: Macmillan, 1980), 119. E.M.W. Tillyard was reminded by VI. 639–655 "of a great baroque painting." *The Miltonic Setting* (London: Chatto & Windus, 1938), 100.

62. *John Milton: A Reader's Guide to his Poetry* (New York: Farrar & Straus, 1963), 255.

63. *MLQ* 27 (1966), 185–196.

64. *The Return of Eden* (Toronto: University of Toronto Press, 1965), 25.

65. To give one reference not in Revard: Martz, *The Paradise Within* (New Haven: Yale University Press, 1964), 124. Greenwood in Newton found the Messiah's victory after three days "plainly alludes to the circumstances of his death and resurrection" (note at l. 748).

66. See Revard's bibliographical note 12, 20.

67. *PMLA*, 87 (1972), 4, part of Jason Rosenblatt's summary of his article, "Structural Unity and Temporal Concordance: The War in Heaven in *Paradise Lost*," 31–41.

68. John M. Steadman, *Milton's Epic Characters* (Chapel Hill: University of North Carolina Press, 1968), 10.

69. *Milton and the English Revolution* (London: Faber & Faber, 1977), 371 ff. Less definite is "political allegory," Revard's grouping (note 20, 26) for analyses by Jackie Di Salvo, Boyd M. Berry, Joan S. Bennett.

70. *Milton: A Structural Reading* (London: Edward Arnold, 1974), 131–132.

71. *A Reading of "Paradise Lost"* (Oxford: Oxford University Press, 1965), 67.

72. *Ibid.* Hanford, "Milton and the Art of War," 214; also *A Milton Handbook*, 2d ed. (New York: Crofts, 1933), 185; B.A. Wright, *Milton's "Paradise Lost"* (New York: Methuen, 1962), 131; Michael Wilding, *Milton's "Paradise Lost"* (Sydney: Sydney University Press, 1969), 73; Revard, "Milton's Critique of Heroic Warfare in *Paradise Lost* V and VI," *SEL* 7 (1967), 119–139; also *The War in Heaven*, 191, 271. What of Homer? "The *Iliad* obviously and unanswerably questions the value of the Trojan war. Hector and Achilles are the poem's heroes because they are both the most valorous and the most unwilling warriors. Helen, as the cause of the war, regrets her fate. The whole middle section of the *Iliad*, seen by many critics as too long drawn–out and repetitious, performs the function of beating in upon our consciousness, in unsparing detail, the repetitious horror of warfare." Joan Malory Webber, *Milton and His Epic Tradition* (Seattle: University of Washington Press, 1979), 39.

73. Freeman, 5. Armor and swords hardly prove Milton's anti-militarism, since he gives them to the good angels also. Indeed Freeman expresses "surprise" when, contrary to his theory, "Michael, God's faithful retainer, appears before Adam dressed like a soldier" (217). Relegated to a footnote (23, 195) is the concession: "Milton's own thoughts on a just war are found in C.D.2. 17. As *PL* 6 shows, he realized that war was sometimes necessary." Much better balanced is Freeman's article, "Milton's Views on War," for *A Milton Encyclopedia*, VIII, 151–155.

74. Mohl, *John Milton and his Commonplace Book* (New York: Frederick Ungar, 1969), 251, quoting *Works*, XVII, 411.

75. *The Burning Oracle* as reprinted in *Poets of Action* (London: Methuen, 1967), 46.

76. "We have orders of the day, a hierarchy, exact submission, extra duties, disputes, regulated ceremonials, prostrations, etiquette, furbished arms, arsenals, depots of chariots and ammunition." H.A. Taine, *History of English Literature* (New York: Grosset & Dunlap, 1908), I, ii. 307. Freeman quotes this, 13.

77. See Le Comte, *Yet Once More: Verbal and Psychological Pattern in Milton* (New York: Liberal Arts Press, 1953), 8–9.

78. "On Translating Homer," *Essays* (London: Oxford University Press, 1914), 287.

79. For psychoanalysis see Michael Lieb, *The Dialectics of Creation: Patterns of Birth and Regeneration in "Paradise Lost"* (Amherst: University of Massachusetts Press, 1970), 120–121.

80. John Philips in R.S. Crane, ed., *A Collection of English Poems, 1660–1800* (New York: Harper, 1932), 313.

81. Cf. William McQueen, "*Paradise Lost* V, VI: The War in Heaven," *SP*, 71 (1974), 89–104; James G. Mengert, "Styling the Strife of Glory: The War in Heaven," *Milton S*, 14 (1980), 95–115.

82. On punning by good characters see Le Comte, *Dictionary of Puns*, viii.

83. *Theogony*, 687 ff., trans. C.A. Elton in *Greek Literature in Translation*, ed., George Howe and G.A. Harrer (New York: Harper, 1924), 85.

84. *Iliad*, trans. Richmond Lattimore (Chicago: University of Chicago Press, 1951), 248. Going from *Iliad* XII to *Iliad* XI would fit a pattern of reverse source adaptation noted by Grant McColley, "Milton's Technique of Source Adaptation," *SP*, 35 (1938), 61–110. In the background is the "epic marvelous" as exemplified by Achilles' rout of Hector and Odysseus' massacre of the suitors. See Steadman, *Epic and Tragic Structure in "Paradise Lost"* (Chicago: University of Chicago Press, 1976), 110–113. A Milton desiring a less warlike effect for his symbolic chariot from Ezekiel, the Merkabah of the Logos, might have taken a hint from Achilles' devastating shout under the aegis of Athene, XVIII. 217 ff. Again at XII he starts out metaphorical (386 ff.) and turns physical (451 ff.).

85. *Chariot of Wrath* (London: Faber & Faber, 1942), 158.

86. Shumaker, *Unpremeditated Verse* (Princeton: Princeton University Press, 1967), 104–132; *Cambridge Milton*, V–VI ed., Robert Hodge and Isabel G. MacCaffrey (1975). Pertinent, too, is the observation by Frederic Jameson (brought to my attention by Edward Tayler): "unlike prose narrative, artificial epic takes as its object of representation not events and actions themselves but rather the describing of them: the process whereby such narrative raw materials are fixed and immobilized in the heightened and embellished speech of verse. There is thus already present in epic discourse a basic and constitutive rift between form and content, between the words and their objects." *Fables of Aggression* (Berkeley: University of California Press, 1979), 76. The latest apology for VI is Lieb's: "When Milton came to celebrate the armies of God in epic form, he had at his disposal an entire tradition of holy war ideology that assimilated the theme of scorn and made it uniquely his own." *Poetics of the Holy* (Chapel Hill: University of North Carolina Press, 1981), 282. For a useful biographical–historical analysis by a military expert, see Robert F. Fallon, *Captain or Colonel: The Soldier in Milton's Life and Art* (Columbia: University of Missouri Press, 1984). One hears of political allegory but nothing like the following from a prettily

illustrated Milanese import: "Among...somewhat odder opinions was Walter Bagehot, claiming that Milton's angels were meant to be the Cavaliers, God the King of England, and the devils the Roundheads." [S. Toulson], *Milton*, "Giants of Literature" (Maidenhead: Sampson Low, 1977), 128. Needless to say, nothing approaching this is to be found in Bagehot's essay on Milton in his *Literary Studies*, which is on a par for utter--or "odder"-- confusion with the information on the next page: "T.S. Eliot, the English–born poet and playwright who settled in America."

87. *A Dictionary of Puns*, xvi.
88. Lawrence W. Hyman, "The Ambiguity of *Paradise Lost* and Contemporary Critical Theory," *Milton Q*, 13 (1979), 1–6; David Aers and Bob Hodge, "'Rational Burning': Milton on Sex and Marriage," *Milton S*, 13 (1979), 3–33; John R. Mulder, "'Ambiguous Words and Jealousies': A Secular Reading of *Paradise Lost*," *Milton S*, 13 (1979), 145–179. Broadbent had used the word "ambivalence" in 1960, 219.
89. *From Virgil to Milton* (London: Macmillan, 1945)236.
90. On parody going back to Elegia III, see below, "Sly Milton: The Meaning Lurking in the Contexts of His Quotations." I cannot agree with Riggs (122) that Milton is deliberately calling attention throughout VI to the impossibility of his self–assigned task: "This brazening of inadequacy can only be meant to convey one thing: in a fallen world one must build with fallen materials."
91. Oliver Elton, *A Survey of English Literature, 1730–1780* (New York: Macmillan, 1928), I, 353.
92. Greenlaw, "A Better Teacher than Aquinas," *SP*, 14 (1917), 213, quoted and commented on by Waldock, 5–9.

WHAT DOUGLAS BUSH STOOD FOR

Miltonists tend to live long, I am glad to note. Is there something sustaining in their author? By way of anecdote: since *A Milton Encyclopedia* has entries only for the deceased, the editors had to find out whether D.H. Stevens, the bibliographer, was still alive. He had been born so long ago that it was hard to believe that he was. But he was, thus failing to qualify for the "Sm–Z" volume that was published in 1980. The Milton scholars who reached eighty and more include David Masson and Alfred Stern in the 19th century, and in our century James Holly Hanford, William Haller, Harris Fletcher, Marjorie Nicolson, Charles G. Osgood, Walter Clyde Curry, and Sir Herbert Grierson. Maurice Kelley is eighty–eight. Allan H. Gilbert became a centenarian. Kelley was the editor of the last volume of the Yale Prose, 1982. Gilbert, last time I saw him – which was admittedly quite a few years ago – had just come back from jogging. Gilbert wrote an essay on how not to be old that I passed on to Douglas Bush.

John Nash Douglas Bush, Gurney Professor of English Literature Emeritus at Harvard University, died of pneumonia March 2, 1983. He was nineteen days short of his eighty–seventh birthday. My sorrow at the ending of our long association, perhaps it would not be presumptuous to call it a friendship (it was not an intimacy), is tempered by the reflection that he not only lived long but retained his faculties to the end. It was almost comic when, during our telephone conversations, Douglas would complain of his waning powers, while simultaneously giving witty proof in his immaculately typed letters and his continuing publications that just the opposite was the case. I, twenty years younger, kept telling him that his memory was better than mine. His son Geoffrey said that, for as far back as he could remember, his father complained of waning powers—— and of course it was never so

The obituary of Douglas Bush in the *New York Times* was a disgrace for a newspaper of record. It was four days late, it lacked a photo, it was parsimonious, it spent half its small space on inept quotation

25

instead of facts, and it was inaccurate. That paper, whose editors apparently do not look at the *Boston Globe*, caught up with the news only after a memorial service was held at the Appleton Memorial Chapel in Harvard Yard. *Time* magazine did him more justice when, in its issue of March 28, it ran an essay on great teachers by Roger Rosenblatt, a former student and colleague.

Bush started life as a Canadian, born in Morrisburg, Ontario, March 21, 1896. At the University of Toronto, where he received his bachelor's degree in 1920 and his master's degree in 1921, he majored in classics, as a Renaissance scholar should (though scarcely any do nowadays). After receiving his Ph.D. from Harvard only two years afterward, he went to England in 1923/24 on a Sheldon traveling fellowship, then he taught at Harvard for three years before transferring to the University of Minnesota, whose press brought out his first book. On September 3, 1927, he married Hazel Cleaver, who lived on to ninety-five. He was at the University of Minnesota from 1927 to 1936, rising rapidly through the ranks to full professor. One of his students there was the biographer Marchette Chute. Harvard called Bush back in 1936; he succeeded to the Gurney chair in 1957 and retired in 1966. At his retirement there was not the usual festschrift but rather a presentation to him of a collection of his essays entitled *Engaged and Disengaged*. I recall that the daily *New York Times* did a review of that (at least), with photo. Collecting this volume of essays instead of compiling a festschrift guaranteed that the book would be well written.

Before going into corroborative detail, let me state, flat out, that Douglas Bush was recognized as the world's outstanding authority on Renaissance English literature and on Milton. In addition, he roamed the centuries in his teaching and in his publications, from Chaucer to Lionel Trilling. He had a special affection for the nineteenth century. With his capacious memory, he could teach the Victorian novel, for example, at a moment's notice. Among his score of books were magisterial studies of Keats, Jane Austen, and Matthew Arnold (utterly disparate figures, of course); he edited, and planned a book on, Tennyson, but it was never completed. By comparison, other eminent scholars seem confined and their production small.

I was middle-aged before I met Bush at a Milton Society dinner. My three degrees are from Columbia, where I taught for half my career. But my contact with Bush's mind came early. I dedicated a 1978 book to Bush as one "whose lectures I was never so fortunate as to hear, but who has taught me in all other ways, beginning forty years ago." When I was a junior at Columbia College, I bought Bush's first book and soon after bought his newly published second. In a way, this kind of beginning has advantages over the cult of personality--especially as Bush in person made no effort to be imposing--which has students gawking at a "name" professor, none of whose publications they have read or intend to read.

They just sit in the classroom and expect to be entertained, they witen not how.

As a writer Bush was as entertaining as he was learned, a rare phenomenon among professors. His humor and wit lighten the heavy task he set for himself in those first two books, *Mythology and the Renaissance Tradition in English Poetry* (1932) and *Mythology and the Romantic Tradition in English Poetry* (1937). Imagine, as just the preliminary requirement, going through the complete works of hundreds of English and, finally, American poets (including, as acknowledged, "some very small beer"), with all the accumulated commentary, and being armed with knowledge, in the original languages, of the poets' sources. Then there was the necessity (for Bush had high standards) of saying something in each individual case that is both fresh and judicious. It adds up to 1,007 pages, not counting the prefaces.

The prefaces should, however, be counted, for Bush's unmistakable voice was there from the very beginning of his huge undertaking. The opening words were:

> This study set out, with Elizabethan confidence, to describe the uses of mythology in English non–dramatic poetry from the Middle Ages to the present. The result of such an ambition can perhaps be suggested in the apt words of a university poet concerning Actaeon: "His hands were changed to feet, and he in short/ Became a stag." In plain prose, this volume ends at 1680; I hope in another volume to complete the tale.

The beginning of the second paragraph of the introduction can serve as an illustration of the author's characteristic sense of paradox and balance, the skill at making a point, even an epigram, without skewing––or skewering––the truth:

> Poetry is largely a matter of symbol, and the complete rebel, like Blake, who flouts tradition and insists on making his own symbols, may achieve originality of a kind, but at a high price, as the most ardent devotee of the prophetic books must admit. The greatest artists, I think Mr. Clive Bell has remarked, always look forward. It is equally true that they always look backward. Of course feeble poets who try to write in a great tradition remain feeble poets, and the bright world of classic myth has allured a number of persons who, in the words of Coleridge, mistake an intense desire to possess the reputation of poetic genius for the actual powers.

There are gems on every page. I soon had occasion to quote the throwaway line about the Elizabethans: "They display a medieval readiness to tell all they know up to the date of publication." One remark, as revised in the Alexander Lectures at the University of Toronto, which were published as *The Renaissance and English Humanism* (1939), reacted to Jesus' scorn for Greek literature in *Paradise Regained*: "It is painful indeed to watch Milton turn and rend some main roots of his being." Those vivid words became a subject, or object, of controversy and elicited many an article.

My teacher at Columbia, Gilbert Highet, in his own monumental book *The Classical Tradition*, called the *Renaissance Tradition* volume "an indispensable work written with fine taste and extensive knowledge." He added of the sequel: "This book is quite as gracefully written as its predecessor, but labours a little under the effort of covering *all* the poets who fall within the period and the pattern. Still, it is nearly always a pleasure and a profit to read."

Bush's mythology books gave sustenance to my particular interests as a student, which were Keats, and Milton, and myth. I was an old-school boy in that I went to Trinity (founded in 1709) in New York, where I had four years of Latin, three of Greek, and three of French. In college I continued those languages and added German and Italian. I was uncertain whether to specialize in the nineteenth century or the seventeenth, but I knew I wanted to get out of the twentieth. As a junior I did a term paper on Keats's *Endymion* for the formidable Emery Neff, who treated undergraduates as graduates. He gave me an unheard of "A plus." If I had received just a plain "A," my academic career might have been different. The result was that I did my master's degree essay on a passage in *Comus*, but returned to Keats as the principal reason for my doctoral dissertation, published in 1944 as *Endymion in England: The Literary History of a Greek Myth*. My second sentence referred––I might better say, deferred––to Bush. Originally it was the first sentence, but an adviser said that was de trop. The master gave it his blessing in a review in the *Journal of English and Germanic Philology* in 1945.

In the same year Bush published his fourth and fifth books, one short, one long, both major (Would he ever do a minor book? we asked). *English Literature in the Earlier Seventeenth Century, 1600–1660* has never had a rival. It is a mine of sometimes very recondite information and a miracle of evenhanded, well-proportioned treatment of major and minor figures and their historical and cultural milieu––everything expected of a textbook and a reference work with the addition of immense readability. The author confined his individualism to style, unlike C.S. Lewis (I am not denying his genius) whose eccentric volume for the sixteenth century in the same Oxford History of English Literature series gives Gavin Douglas four times more space than Donne. Bush's first thirty-eight pages, "The Background of the Age," show his power of synthesizing. In 1962 he made elaborate changes for a second edition, just as, the next year, he revised *Mythology and the Renaissance Tradition*. Modest, he never felt he had said the last word. I had a startling instance of this when he wrote a foreword for a 1973 book of mine. He said if I was not satisfied with his comment, he would revise it. Another time, I remarked that I was pleased I had as many as forty–five students in my Milton course at Albany. Since I was sometimes lucky to have a dozen, I was not being boastful but exuberant. Then I asked him (he had retired) how many he had been accustomed to. He did not want to tell me, but finally said "about 250"--which was probably an understatement. An instance of his irony is buried in his 1962 bibliography on Donne, where he observed of a promise still not kept that a scholar's "long–awaited edition of the letters will be valuable for those who live to see it."

One thing could stir this scholar–critic from his even temper: an attack on Milton. "The Modern Reaction Against Milton" was the title of the first four Messenger Lectures delivered at Cornell University, which comprise that other 1945 book, *"Paradise Lost" in Our Time: Some Comments.* (This went out of print so fast that I, then in California, suffered the cultural lag of having to beg the press for a last, damaged copy.) Bush quoted F.R. Leavis's "smug words":

> Milton's dislodgment, in the past decade, after his two centuries of predominance, was effected with remarkably little fuss. The irresistible argument was, of course, Mr. Eliot's creative achievement; it gave his few critical asides--potent, it is true, by context--their finality, and made it unnecessary to elaborate a case.

It takes an effort to remember now what authority T.S. Eliot once wielded as a critic. His critical asides caused tremors, if not earthquakes, that reverberated around the literary world. Bush took him on undaunted, even as he later made short shrift, in a review essay, of my great teacher and colleague Mark Van Doren for displaying imperfect sympathies in regard to the same epic. Ironically, Eliot was to leave Leavis high and dry (he was always dry) by recanting, at least partially, in 1947. Past the polemics, *"Paradise Lost" in Our Time* revived, not the faded "new humanism" of Irving Babbitt, but Christian humanism--so old that it seemed new.

At last a minor work appeared, *The Portable Milton* (1949), which, nevertheless, sold well in hard and soft cover. The editor was not allowed any annotations, only a glossary. This was one Harvard professor, unlike so many in the ivy--or ivory--tower, who was not a snob about reaching a wider audience. To convey a cultural message, I verily believe he would have written for the *Saturday Evening Post.* He was receptive to two popular efforts of mine in seventeenth–century biography, reviewing the one in the *New York Times* and supplying a blurb for the other that spoke (too sanguinely) of "all the ingredients of a best seller." On the other hand, he despised sexual, not to say Freudian, emphasis, and when I did a scholarly book, *Milton and Sex* (the blunt title was not the one I wanted),

I kept it from him. The Columbia University Press made a mistake in sending him my 1981 *Dictionary of Puns in Milton's English Poetry*, which, containing same wild conjectures, strained his good will, but he did his best to give the press something it could quote: "In its special way it is informative, stimulating, and provocative, thanks to the author's acute reading. As he says, one doesn't need to agree with all his findings." His personal letter to me was warmer, but, of course, also honest about his doubts. In a 1978 essay for *Daedalus*, he used, to my surprise, a pun I had thrown his way to complain about literary interpretations that "are mainly or wholly `phallacious.'"

In the 1950s, "as plates dropped from his pocket," Bush's bounty continued: *Science and English Poetry* (1950); *Classical Influences in Renaissance Literature* (1952); editions of Tennyson and Keats and Shakespeare's sonnets (the last with his colleague Alfred Harbage). All the while, starting in the 1920s, he was doing articles and essays and notes and reviews that would have been sufficient to give a reputation to a lesser man; and these continued to the end. He served on many an editorial board, and I shudder to think of the plethora of manuscripts he was asked to evaluate. The last letter I had from him, September 29, 1982, spoke of having "just got embroiled in two troublesome articles on which I was asked to report." Former students insisted on visiting him in his retirement and stayed long. "Each day of the holiday brings an old student for two or three hours, as usual. I do really appreciate such *pietas*, though it becomes a bit overwhelming" (December 31, 1974). Great teachers have to suffer this as gladly as they can.

In my 1961 *Milton Dictionary* I called James Holly Hanford the "dean of American Miltonists" and had no entry for Bush, who had not yet moved massively into Milton, as he was about to do, It was a logical, a natural, development. In 1964 he contributed an elegant critical biography to the Masters of World Literature series (the same auspices for his later *Keats, Matthew Arnold,* and *Jane Austen*). The year 1965 brought (besides the collected *Prefaces to Renaissance Literature*) a delightful surprise, a new edition by Bush of the Houghton Mifflin "Cambridge" *Complete Poetical Works* of Milton. One was not expecting this, since there had already been three Cambridge editions: William Vaughn Moody's in 1899 and 1924 (the latter with revisions by E.K. Rand of Moody's versions of the Latin poetry) and Harris Fletcher's completely new edition in 1941 (and Fletcher was still very much alive in 1965). This time Bush had his footnotes as well as glossary, and separate introductions; he completed the enterprise he had begun with *The Portable Milton*—a fresh translation of the Latin poems (one that put to shame another that had lately appeared wherein the editor, despite the availability of a half-dozen trots, committed one blunder after another). This Cambridge Milton has become standard for the general reader who wants a modernized text.

Bush was on the editorial board for the Yale *Complete Prose Works*, a lumbering, uneven undertaking typical of the platoon approach to scholarship, whereby it is reasoned that two editors must be better than one, and four better than two. (*A Milton Encyclopedia* has 159 contributors.) Bush was not active in the editing, which for volume 7 was so bad that it had to be recalled, like a defective automobile: it took the team six years to reissue it. But Bush was drawn into a parallel project, *A Variorum Commentary on Milton's Poems*, the first since Henry John Todd's in the nineteenth century. Bush's assignment was the Latin (and Greek) poems. He completed it in 1970--361 pages--a stupendous coverage of a relatively neglected area. (Meanwhile, for a general audience, there had been the Jayne Lectures at the American Philosophical Society, published in 1968 as *Pagan Myth and Christian Tradition in English Poetry*.)

There Bush's labors on the *Variorum* had been meant to end. His friend A.S.P. Woodhouse, of the University of Toronto, was working on the minor English poems. But Woodhouse died suddenly in October 1964, and Bush had to take over. In some ways it would have been easier if he had started from scratch. As he wrote: "In general, the effort to revise and complete the work of another man, especially of a very old and much admired friend, has involved endless difficulties." Unfair critics were to jeer at the spectacle of the difference of opinion between the editors: Bush suppressed neither Woodhouse nor himself. Difference of opinion is, in any case, what a variorum is all about. There was also objection that, on a number of long–debated matters, Bush showed where his own preference lay. His reply was that he was not merely a recording machine. He was scrupulous in including whatever, however unlikely, had found its way into print, which is more than can be said for the editor of *Paradise Regained*, who was too enamored of his own views to produce a true variorum.

The three volumes on the minor poems, issued in 1972, came to 1,143 pages. "Lycidas," 193 lines, received 190 pages. Of course that contains the most famous crux in English literature, the problem of what Milton had in mind when he wrote, "But that two–handed engine at the door / Stands ready to smite once and smite no more." Bush analyzed forty–five explanations, based on a bibliography of one hundred items. So much for two lines. *Comus* was given 255 pages, "L'Allegro" and "Il Penseroso," 114.

The teacher of England's second greatest poet, the curious amateur, the readier of an article or a book, was now provided with instant learning. No longer was there any excuse--if ever there had been--for fobbing off as new what, in fact, was old. (But it was also a stimulus to going on from there.) Someone had at last mastered and mustered and absorbed the immense and scattered commentary to date, often from sources available at too few libraries. It is a monument that will endure because it is resorted to all the time.

Of how many can it be said that they can generalize but are also respectful of detail? Quoting Shakespeare, Edward Armstrong remarked that scholars "are temperamentally inclined to be either `of imagination all compact' or `continual plodders.'" The broadsweep people do not descend to footnotes, and the footnoters criticize the others as glib and unsound. In the Winter 1982/83 *American Scholar*, Arthur F. Stocker, writing on Bush's Harvard colleague Edward Kennard Rand, separated "the miners of data, who gather and sort diverse bits of new information that become building blocks out of which the edifices of the future can later be constructed" from the "somewhat rarer folk who can range widely over a broad area of knowledge, and who from extensive personal experience in that field are able to make valid syntheses and to offer securely based interpretations."

Bush was both kinds. No wonder he was an expert on Keats and Tennyson, with their love of a mythical past, and could say with Matthew Arnold, the subject of his 1971 book, "I am bound by my own definition of criticism: a disinterested endeavor to learn and propagate the best that is known and thought in the world."

Characteristic of Bush's quiet generosity is an acknowledgment he wouldn't let me make while he was alive. For my edition of *Justa Edovardo King* I had trouble translating some of the Latin poems, which have a rhetorical extravagance typical of academics. Slyly I asked Douglas––to whom I was dedicating the volume––if he would take a look at the proofs. He did, and found, as I feared, errors, serious errors. (*All* errors are serious––to a scholar.) Then I said, "I hate to trouble you further––but there are also these three tiny Greek poems, and I *know* my Greek is shaky." The result, more corrections, just in time.

The *Times* obituary wrongly stated that the Arnold book was Bush's last. The last was *Jane Austen*, which came out in 1975 (on the two hundredth anniversary of her birth) when he was seventy-nine. Again he had the problem of keeping a clear head above a large body of material. The Janeites are a busy cult. That novelist's "instinct for order and proportion," an instinct "both ethical and artistic," answered to something deep in her critic.

Bush was a conserver, not an innovator. It is interesting that one honor that never came to him was the presidency of the Modern Language Association, nor would he have wanted latterly to hold such a post in an organization that had deteriorated into an umbrella for warring political factions and discussion groups for increasingly bizarre topics. When I resigned (as many scholars did) in 1971, disgusted at the successful maneuvers of a radical clique, Douglas sympathetically noted that he could not make the same protest, because he was a life member.

Bush's six–by–seven–inch stationery was right for an epigrammatic style. In the summers his letters came from Norwich, Vermont, where he owned a farm until it became too difficult for him to make the annual move. He wrote from Cambridge at the beginning of June 1973: "I have just brought back our 1947 Ford from the garage where it was being activated after nine months in dead storage as usual. It is a gallant machine, something between a Lord Mayor's coach and a Brink's truck, which has become a moving landmark around Norwich and Hanover. The annual suspense over the question of its still running always deranges me." Still, he was not too old–fashioned to sit with his wife and watch the Boston Red Sox on television in the home they had bought in 1936 at 3 Clement Circle, Cambridge. There *was* a circular driveway, but of course the weather was far from clement. Clemency was not guaranteed even in Norwich, where in July 1973 they were marooned for a week by a flood that left them a crevasse in place of a lawn and a driveway. But Douglas was as hardy a scholar as I have ever known. When a burglar broke in at Cambridge, Bush, nearing eighty, came down from the bedroom in the middle of the night to investigate––and the culprit fled. Norwich didn't provide total security either: "All our firewood was stolen except a dozen little pieces and I must spend some time and energy gathering branches to be cut up, for mornings are cold and evenings are too cool for comfort. Apart from this and other Edenic activities I seem to have fallen into a loose schedule, reading Plato in the morning, Virgil in the afternoon, and Molière in the evening" (June 15, 1974).

In the introduction to *The Portable Milton*, he said of "Lycidas": "Of the subtle complexity of the texture there is no room to speak here; one begins to understand that, and the theme, only when one knows the poem by heart." Like Marjorie Nicolson, he knew a great deal of poetry by heart. When I dined at Clement Circle in the fall of 1974, he told me that when he could not sleep he went over lines in his mind. He was a natural reader from boyhood, and he had style because the best rubbed off on him. More, to borrow an epigram from his 1976 memorial essay on Lionel Trilling, he was one who "did not live to read but read to live." Of how many can that be said these days? We have professors who cannot write and whose interpretations show they cannot read––and all because they were never amateurs, never lovers. They read only for career reasons, not because they love to read. And they do not read much or move beyond a narrow round where they hope to publish. A liberal education does not, as Cardinal Newman sadly conceded, guarantee character, but it should do something for the mind. Douglas Bush embodied, because he had assimilated, the best of Western civilization.

"Western Civilization"––is that a bias? Bush's manifold contributions predated the ideological revolution in English departments, the full Bloom (Harold, not Allan) of theory, the feminist and multi-ethnic questioning of the canon. But in asides (not broadsides) he anticipated Allan Bloom's conclusion that "our students have lost the practice and taste for reading," Alvin Kernan's that reading books "is ceasing to be the primary way of knowing something in our society."

The last I heard from him was a Christmas card (ten weeks before he died) in response to my having sent him some absurd light verse. Alluding to my retirement he wrote, "Your Miltonic verses seem to indicate a soul rejoicing in new-found freedom." "A soul rejoicing in new-found freedom"--what a meaning that has now!

SATAN'S HERESIES
IN *PARADISE REGAINED*

At the beginning of *Paradise Regained*, Satan, having witnessed Jesus' baptism, calls--like a pope or a prelate--a "council" or "consistory" (I, 40, 42). Church councils, consistories, conclaves--Milton was wont to take a dim view of them, figuratively and literally. They were not a source of clear bright truth; he consigned them to hell. We remember the "secret conclave" of *Paradise Lost* I, 795, an ironic glance at cardinals locked up to elect a pope. As Tillyard remarked, Milton "assumes, in the first book especially, some knowledge of the earlier poem."[1] In neither poem does God ever hold what is called a council. *Council* is a bad word, used only of the bad, in all its nine occurrences.[2]

"Councils," "conclaves," "consistory" are all used with significant contempt at the end of the first book of *Of Reformation*. The second class of hinderers of reform, the libertines, have their own easy substitute for "a consistory." The first class of hinderers, the "antiquitarians," expect someone like Milton to have wasted his precious hours in the endless conferring of councils and conclaves that demolish one another....But I trust they for whom God hath reserved the honor of reforming this church will easily perceive their adversaries' drift in thus calling for antiquity: they fear the plain field of the scriptures; the chase is too hot; they seek the dark, the bushy, the tangled forest, they would imbosk: they feel themselves struck in the transparent streams of divine truth; they would plunge and tumble, and think to lie hid in the foul weeds and muddy waters, where no plummet can reach the bottom.[3]

What is so unplummeted as the bottomless "deep" (*Paradise Regained* I, 90) into which a third of the angels plunged and tumbled? But they were loosed on mankind, "From hell's deep-vaulted den to dwell in light" (I, 116), and are able to hold councils in the notoriously damp region of mid-air. "Council," "dark," and "adversary" are verbal links thirty years after *Of Reformation*:

> the Adversary
>
> . . . .
>
>   in mid-air
> To council summons all his mighty peers,
> Within thick clouds and dark tenfold involved,
> A gloomy cónsistory.   (I,33,39-42)

Barbara Lewalski made in passing an interesting point when she said of the last word that it "initiates the poem's frequent association of Satan with the antichristian Roman church seen as deriving from him."[4] This is the first A.D. council, antedating Nicaea and Constantinople by three centuries. Date it A.D. 30. Call it Infernal I.

Satan summons it to raise a question of "sore" concern. At Jesus' baptism he saw and heard strange things:

>   thence on his head
> A perfect dove descend, whate'er it meant,
> And out of heav'n the Sov'reign Voice I heard.
> "This is my Son beloved, in him am pleased."
> His mother is then mortal, but his Sire
> He who obtains the monarchy of heav'n,
> And what will he not do to advance his Son?
> His first-begot we know, and sore have felt,
> When his fierce thunder drove us to the deep;
> Who this is we must learn, for man he seems
> In all his lineaments, though in his face
> The glimpses of his Father's glory shine.   (I, 82-93)

The devil has touched on the two greatest mysteries of the Christian faith, the Trinity and the Incarnation.[5] "Whate'er it meant." Is the dove the Third Person of the Holy Trinity? We cannot expect Satan to ask, but we have no reason to be complacent. Milton scholars cannot agree on the similar question of whether, in invoking "Thou, Spirit, who led'st this glorious Eremite / Into the desert" (8-9), the poet means the Holy Ghost as Third Person. In the unpublished *De Doctrina Christiana*, Milton is almost as puzzled by the Matthew iii, 16-17, reference as is Satan: "Was this intended as the first revelation of the Spirit to the Church? No: for when it is mentioned nothing is said about it or its function" (YP, VI, 284). On this topic the Infernal Council passes up a capital opportunity to find "no end, in wand'ring mazes lost" (*PL* II, 561).

We ought to keep alert to the fact that Milton can be of the devil's party without uttering it. There was Satan's prior skepticism toward the baptist as one who "in the consecrated stream / Pretends to wash off sin" (*PR* I, 72-73). Milton felt "we are not saved by that outward baptism which washes away merely the filth of the flesh"[6] E.L. Marilla called this harmony of views "an interesting instance, it seems, of the use of the devil to further one's legitimate aims."[7] The devil would not wish to believe that sin can be washed away. Unlike Milton, he has no spiritual apprehension and no understanding of the symbolic; for different reasons, neither put stock in white magic versus black. *Of Reformation* identifies as a symptom of early corruption of the church that baptism was "changed into a kind of exorcism" (the latter preceding the former in Roman Catholic practice).[8] One of this tract's indictments against Constantine was his naive and superstitious postponement of that washing away: "his living unbaptized almost to his dying day."[9] But in *De Doctrina Christiana*, Milton himself was far from orthodox. His "position on this sacrament may be described as Socinian–Anabaptist immersionism, with the further stipulation that the rite must be performed in running water."[10]

The author, then, becomes a distracting presence in the background. But our eye ought to be fixed mainly on the arch heretic, the heretic of heretics. The devil has not been given his due as a would–be theologian. He, for personal reasons, wants to determine the nature of the God–man and the Father–Son relationship. He knows already that in some sense "Son of God" is a correct title for Jesus. How obsessively––or persistently––often it is sounded (in a double sense––repeated and probed)! "The phrase `Son of God' occurs no less than 39 times; 10 times in Book I and 21 times in the concluding book."[11] It is a fixed epithet, but also a point of debate. Milton wrestled with it in *De Doctrina*. It is the rock, or the sphinx, against which the Tempter or attempter hurls himself in the smaller epic. In the words of Woodhouse, "Beside its primary theme of Christ as the second Adam, *Paradise Regained* has a secondary theme, namely, the nature and office of the Son of God, significantly mentioned in the prelude."[12]

Woodhouse, however, proceeds to undercut his statement by declining to believe that Satan really has the doubt about Christ's identity that he expresses to his followers. Satan is not even given latitude for wishful thinking. Both Allen and MacKellar take this posture too, although it eviscerates the poem, empties it of drama.[13] It also goes against tradition. "During both Middle Ages and Renaissance, it was widely assumed that his chief object in attempting to seduce Christ was to find out if he really were the Son of God."[14] Father of lies Satan is, but I take it that at Infernal I he is telling no less than the agonized truth and has uncovered the spring of all his subsequent action. Here I am agreeing with––to name recent commentators only––Bush, Muir, Cleveland, Daiches, Stein, Williamson, Lewalski, Hunter, and Weber.[15]

Jesus' words cited for the opposite view are ambiguous:[16] "Why dost thou then suggest to me distrust,/ Knowing who I am, as I know who thou art?" (I, 355–56). Carey comments: "`Knowing who I am' can merely mean `Knowing that I am the Son of God': in this sense Satan knows who Christ is: what worries him is the meaning of that title."[17]

I comment that Jesus is probably teasing his opponent. "Knowing" can be conditional: "*if* you know." (Compare Fowler on "Refusing," *PL* II, 452.)[18] Harder it is to say what Jesus as man knows, but Milton has gone to great lengths--the whole length of his poem, indeed--to stress the Tempter's tortured uncertainty. Suspicion he has: "So to subvert whom he suspected raised / To end his reign on earth so long enjoyed" (I, 124-25). Hope he is supposed to have lost, but he hopes his worst suspicions are wrong. The *Variorum Commentary* editor reasons that this leader "must try to encourage" his followers. "To do so he resorts to the pretence of doubting who Christ is."[19] What sort of encouragement is it that leaves the audience filled "with deep dismay" at "his words" (I, 108-106)? Such an explanation does not explain. Surely Satan would have done a better job of lying than that. Jesus says of him, "Lying is thy sustenance, thy food" (429), but his words on this occasion sustain neither him nor "th'infernal crew." In fact he has blurted out all his distress, which they now share. (At the second council he is equally frank, and equally depressing.)

Coleridge got into trouble for declaring in a lecture "that Milton had represented Satan as a sceptical Socinian."[20] Actually this demon does not know what to think. Had he had a chance to read the first thirty-six lines of *Paradise Regained* he wouldn't have been helped, for they contain two references to Jesus as man (I,4,36), two references to him as son of God (11, 32), and one to him as "the son of Joseph" (23). The fallen angel no longer has the mental equipment to grasp celestial mysteries. He has become gross, with common sense (and wishful thinking) his only guide. Water obviously cannot wash off sins. A dove is "perfect"--for eating. This is serpent's wisdom ("snaky wiles," 120). "His first-begot we know" (89)--and this son of God is not likely to be the same one. God has many sons. Adam was one. Satan himself is, or was, another. (He affirms to Jesus, *PR* IV, 518, what he denied to Abdiel, *PL* V, 853ff.) If Jesus were by any chance to be called "second Adam" (*PL* XI, 383), that cannot mean he is first son. That would violate chronology and common sense.

"Accordingly let no one expect me to preface what I have to say with a long metaphysical introduction, or bring into my argument all that play-acting of the persons of the godhead." Who is this who is so impatient with theology? Not Satan--but Milton, in *De Doctrina Christiana*.[21] MacKellar's note on *PR* I, 60-61, reads: Satan "does not understand the meaning of the curse, because the literalness of his mind always prevents his grasping the meaning of a metaphor." Satan, Milton, *Paradise Regained*--all have been called Arian. And what epigram has diagnosed the basic trouble with Arius, the fourth-century heresiarch? "He could not understand a metaphor."[22]

But the poet understands some metaphors, at least, and soon leaves his character Satan to wallow alone in heresy. The first is the Military

Messiah heresy. At Infernal I Satan sees God as a monarch who will now become aggressive (therefore dangerous) because he has a full-grown son, or prince, for whom, or by whom, new territory must be won. "And what will he not do to advance his Son" (I, 88). He will wage war. "Ye see our danger on the utmost edge / Of hazard" (94–95). That edge is *acies*, the "perilous edge / Of battle" of *PL* I, 276–77. Something must be done "Ere in the head of nations he appear / Their king, their leader, and supreme on earth" (*PR* I, 98–99).

This is a mistaken view of the Christ as general and temporal king that must be corrected. It was widely held among the Jews, chafing under centuries of oppression. The "Plain fishermen" of Galilee give it plangent voice as they long for Jesus' return for the wrong reason (*PR* II, 31ff). Within a hundred lines of the dissolution of Infernal I the didactic poet replies. He presents Jesus as having contemplated such action in his youth—and having decided against it:

> Victorious deeds
> Flamed in my heart, heroic acts: one while
> To rescue Israel from the Roman yoke,
> Then to subdue and quell o'er all the earth
> Brute violence and proud tyrannic pow'r,
> Till truth were freed, and equity   restored;
> Yet held it more humane, more heavenly, first
> By winning words to conquer willing hearts,
> And make persuasion do the work of fear.
> (I, 215–23)

The lines are notable for being made of whole cloth, without basis in the Gospels. This was self-temptation, but Satan had the same idea, and when he tempts Jesus to join the Parthians against Rome, we can speculate that he has returned to the Military Messiah heresy as a diversion. Whatever supernatural force the son of God has, let others bear its brunt, not him

If Jesus is a mere man and unfit to be a Military Messiah, Satan will offer him delusions of grandeur that can end in disaster. The Parthians had already proved themselves totally unreliable allies (not that Satan would tell).[23] As for the near future, Milton had readers who would readily recall the circumstances attending the fall of Jerusalem a mere forty years later. Jesus himself spoke of the false oracles: "But what have been thy answers, what but dark, / Ambiguous, and with double sense deluding" (*PR* I, 434–35). Josephus tells of the messianic hopes that deluded the Jews into taking on the Roman legions:

> But now, what did most elevate them in undertaking this war, was an ambiguous oracle that was also found in their sacred writings, how, "about that time, one from their country should become

governor of the habitable earth." The Jews took this prediction to belong to themselves in particular; and many of the wise men were thereby deceived in their determination. Now, this oracle certainly denoted the government of Vespasian, who was appointed emperor in Judea. However, it is not possible for men to avoid fate, although they see it beforehand. But these men interpreted some of these signals according to their own pleasure; and some of them they utterly despised, until their madness was demonstrated, both by the taking of their city and their own destruction.[24]

The sincerity of Satan's military offer is suspected by Jesus, who instances the near destruction of Jerusalem (1 Chronicles xxi, 17)[25] a thousand years before:

> But whence to thee this zeal? Where was it then
> For Israel, or for David, or his throne,
> When thou stood'st up his tempter to the pride
> Of numb'ring Israel, which cost the lives
> Of threescore and ten thousand Israelites
> By three days' pestilence? Such was thy zeal
> To Israel then, the same that now to me.
>
> (III, 407–13)

Repeated "zeal" makes an association with Zealots, those futile resisters of Roman rule.

So far we have seen Satan (1) bemused by the rite of baptism, (2) puzzled over Jesus' nature, and (3) mistaking Jesus' mission. Satan will persist in all these kinds of errors. The problem of Jesus' nature dogs Infernal Council II, where an issue is raised that was not officially settled until the Council of Chalcedon, A.D. 451. Satan admits he does not know "If he [Jesus] be man by mother's side at least, / With more than human gifts from Heaven adorned" (II, 136–37). Editors unwarrantably take the comma that appears in the original after "least" and put it after "side," changing the meaning. The result is an opportunity for theological debate comparable to inserting or removing an iota in *homo(i)ousion*. If the comma is placed after "side," Satan is committing the Docetist heresy of denying any human parentage to Christ. The god appeared on earth only as a phantasm; his sufferings and death were mere appearance. "If he suffered he was not God. If he was God he did not suffer." Or possibly the Apollinarian heresy is being advanced, which, at the very least, emphasized the divinity of Christ at the expense of his full manhood.

Having no other guide, I follow Milton's original text, which implies the opposite heresy, to wit, that both of Jesus' parents were human, that he was just a man, but superlatively endowed. This is the Gnostic or Ebionite heresy:

> A certain Cerinthus also in Asia taught that the world was not made by the first God, but by a certain Virtue far separated and removed from the Principality which is above all things, a Virtue which knows not the God over all. He added that Jesus was not born of a virgin but was the son of Joseph and Mary, like many other men, but superior to all others in justice, prudence and wisdom.[26]

Perhaps we are in the presence of "a modified form of ebionism"[27] known as dynamic monarchianism. William B. Hunter, Jr. opts for this in his look at "the monarchy of heav'n" (I, 87) passage.[28] Whatever the label, Satan's inference is that his human opponent is exceptional only as was "The first and wisest" (IV, 293) of the Greek philosophers, Socrates (Jean Balzac's "Socrate chrestien"), and so may yet reveal weaknesses, though they will not be for women (Belial's crude proposal). Satan is still promulgating the heresy near the end of the poem when he spits out "virgin-born" sarcastically: "Then hear, O son of David, virgin-born, / For Son of God to me is yet in doubt" (IV, 500-01). Only with the miracle of the pinnacle are he and his doubts struck down.

Opposite to the Military Messiah heresy about Christ's mission is a heresy that opens his mercy too widely. Alexander Ross made it sound current by mentioning it in his much reprinted *Pansebeia*: "Some say the devils shall be saved."[29] Satan tries that out on Jesus:

> to that gentle brow
> Willingly I could fly, and hope thy reign,
> From that placid aspéct and meek regard,
> Rather than aggravate my evil state,
> Would stand between me and thy Father's ire
> (Whose ire I dread more than the fire of hell),
> A shelter and a kind of shading cool
> Interposition, as a summer's cloud.
>
>   (III, 215-22)

It is just a hovering—and a flattering—over an interesting alternative. The word "brow" is a surprise: it is as if the Devil started to say—as if Milton started to say—"breast," but drew back from the tenderness of it. We see the normal usage in Barnabe Barnes' line, "To fly for refuge to thy wounded breast."[30] Most of Satan's speech makes clear that "all hope is lost / Of my reception into grace" (III, 204-05). The rationale, the correct doctrine, is given in Book III of *Paradise Lost*: "The first sort by their own suggestion fell, / Self-tempted, self-depraved; man falls deceived / By the other first; man therefore shall find grace, / The other none" (129-32). Besides, Satan is long past the possibility of repentance.

But there were tender-hearted theologians in the early church—Clement of Alexandria, Origen, St. Gregory of Nyssa—who argued that even the devils will ultimately share in the grace of salvation. This heresy is called Apocatastasis.[31] It was formally condemned at Constantinople II, A.D. 553.

Besides formal heresies, two insidious moral errors are introduced that need special labeling and can be loosely accounted heresies. Satan puts one forward in the first temptation:

> But if thou be the Son of God, command
> That out of these hard stones be made thee bread;
> So shalt thou save thyself and us relieve
> With food, whereof we wretched seldom taste. (I, 342–45)

Here is the sinful-means-to-good-end heresy. What price bread for the needy? What a humane, what a charitable, what a Salvation Army proposal, to "us relieve / With food, whereof we wretched seldom taste." One can hear the hypocritical whine. (In prose Milton decided it was wrong to give alms to wandering beggars!)[32] Save yourself, that you may save others: it is seemingly a Christian message, like that of *The Pilgrim's Progress*. But performing the miracle would be committing the sin of "distrust" (I, 355) of God's providence: "(as we be slanderously reported, and as some affirm that we say,) Let us do evil, that good may come?" (Romans iii, 8). The Angelic Doctor repeated St. Paul's warning: "Evil should not be done in order that good may result."[33] Sin is the only evil. But some Jesuits of Milton's day took the position that the end justifies the means. "A man may seek out an occasion [of sin], directly and out of set purpose (*primo & per se*) when the spiritual or temporal concernment of himself or his neighbor inclines him thereto." So reads a quotation in a 1658 book that initials indicate Milton owned, a translation of Blaise Pascal's *Provincial Letters*.[34] In his *Medulla Theologiae Moralis* of 1650, which had gone through forty-five editions by 1670, the German Jesuit Hermann Busembaum asserted, "Cum finis est licitus, etiam media sunt licita."[35] ("When the end is lawful, the means are also lawful.") The work was finally officially condemned in France when it was found to encourage assassination and regicide. Milton's past references to Jesuits consist of the usual English Protestant deprecations.[36] His upbringing was, as Parker noted, "Jesuit-hating."[37] I gather that he, like Donne (*Ignatius His Conclave*) and Phineas Fletcher (*Locustae, vel Pietas Jesuitica*), would not have minded conjoining Satan and a Jesuit, or Jesuitical casuistry, even as the teen-aged poet allied the Prince of Darkness (darkness includes sophistry) and the pope in *In Quintum Novembris*, with the Jesuit Garnett in the historical background. The *Commonplace Book* and *Areopagitica* pointed to the ethical problem (*Of Education* called it after Aristotle, *proairesis* [CM, IV, 284]), of what a cunning mixture good and evil are: "those confused seeds which were imposed upon Psyche [Greek for soul] as an incessant labor to cull out, and sort asunder, were not more intermixed."[138] The *Commonplace Book* opens with a stunningly appropriate quotation from Tertullian: "the devil steeps whatever deadly dish he prepares in God's dearest...benefits."[39] That metaphor becomes literal in the first temptation, as we would expect of the materialistic Adversary.

Finally, still in the area of the edible and bearing on the last of the heresies, there has been endless discussion of the relation between the first temptation and the banquet scene. Does the latter "inartistically" repeat the former "in other terms"? Or is the banquet "the first phase of the second temptation and completely distinct from the first"?[40] Charles Lamb complained, "The mighty artillery of sauces, which the cook–fiend conjures up, is out of proportion to the simple wants and plain hunger of the guest."[41] Mark Van Doren commented, "There is Milton blundering again."[42] No, there is Satan blundering again. He *would* think that a sumptuous feast, with pretty attendants of both sexes, should have an effect (as it does on every *homme moyen sensuel*), where plain bread did not. He has offered up, whether to man or god, his very best. He is genuinely surprised at the rejection:

> That I have also power to give thou seest;
> If of that pow'r I bring thee voluntary
> What I might have bestowed on whom I pleased,
> And rather opportunely in this place
> Chose to impart to thy apparent need,
> Why shouldst thou not accept it? But I see
> What I can do or offer is suspect.
>
> (II, 393–99)

I shall call this the Pharisaic heresy (cf. *PL* XII, 533–35). It is the belief that, if the externals of an offering are right, nothing else counts. Offer up a meal fit for a god, offer up what (according to the Hollywood joke) "God could do if he had a lot of money," and the god must find it acceptable. It is not to the point to inquire, as the Lady of *Comus* and Jesus do, about the nature or motivation of the giver. The only kind of fair question is whether the Setian wine is of the best vintage, the myrrhine cup spotless, and the lobster (if such be not "unclean," which it is) boiled to perfection. Satan hasn't read *De Doctrina Christiana*, which explains: "Also opposed to true religion is hypocritical worship, where the external forms are duly observed, but without any internal or spiritual involvement. This is extremely offensive to God" (YP, VI, 667).

Satan could have remembered what happened to the plainer offering of the one whom some of the rabbis identified as his son by Eve, Cain.[43] The Book of Genesis is silent as to why the Lord "had respect unto Abel and to his offering" and "had not respect" unto Cain's (iv, 4–5). Surely the answer is not that the Lord prefers meat to produce. As Cowley said, "It is hard to guess what it was in *Cains sacrifice* that displeased *God*."[44] Milton has to interpolate an explanation: Cain "was not sincere" (*PL* XI, 443). The editors are silent on what precedent, if any, the poet had for his (characteristic) rationalization, but the Geneva Bible of 1560 carried the marginal note, "Because he was an hypocrite and offred onely for an outwarde shew without sinceritie of heart."[45] In short, two offerings four thousand years apart are rejected by the Lord for the same reason. As for "outwarde shew," Adam hopes he will never be beguiled by that in Eve (*PL* VIII, 538).

To summarize, in *Paradise Regained* Satan holds imitation church councils and touches on points of dogma and mysteries that troubled early Christians and that Milton struggled with in *De Doctrina Christiana*. Is Jesus God or man or both? What is his relation to the Father? Is he the Military Messiah? Can and will he save the devil? What about baptism? Does a good end justify sinful means, and what constitutes an acceptable offering? All the wrong answers can be labeled and have been long since condemned by majority vote (though they have a way of cropping up again—for example, the Socinian Racovian Catechism which Milton was called to account for licensing in 1652 and which was ordered burned).[46] Quite apart from his deliberate deceptions and lies, "his weak arguing and fallacious drift" (*PR* III, 4), Satan is confusing and confused, a would-be Christologist who grapples with some real problems—and loses. Things of the spirit are beyond him, and the only way to convince him of anything (*convince* means *conquer*) is to (not for the first time) knock him down. St. Paul said it: "But the natural man receiveth not the things of the Spirit of God: for they are foolishness unto him: neither can he know them, because they are spiritually discerned" (I Corinthians ii, 14). Jesus said it: "Get thee behind me, Satan: thou art an offence unto me; for thou savourest not the things that be of God, but those that be of men" (Matthew xvi, 23; cf. Mark viii, 33).

NOTES

1. E.M.W. Tillyard, *Milton* (New York: Collier, 1967), 254.
2. Of the fallen angels: *PL* I, 755; II, 20, 506; VI, 416, 507; X, 428; *PR* I, 40; II, 118; of the opponents of Enoch: *PL* XI, 661. At twenty–one, Milton wrote of the Son as "wont at Heav'ns high Councel–table, / To sit the midst of Trinal Unity" (Nativity hymn, 10–11), but that was under the influence of Phineas Fletcher: "that Trine–one with himself in councell sits." See A.S.P. Woodhouse and Douglas Bush, ed., *Variorum Commentary* on *The Minor English Poems* (New York: Columbia University Press, 1972), II, 65. Hereafter, to escape such a misleading spelling in the original texts as *Counsel*, I quote Milton's poetry and prose in modernized form: for the poetry, *Complete Poetical Works*, ed., Bush (Boston: Houghton Mifflin, 1965). The unfavorable references to councils in the prose can be readily traced through Frank A. Patterson and French R. Fogle, *Index*, 2 vols. (New York, 1940) to the Columbia edition of the *Works*, ed., Patterson et al., 18 vols. (New York, 1931–38), hereafter cited as CM.
3. Frank A. Patterson, ed., *The Student's Milton* (New York: Crofts, 1933), 453, 454 (CM, III, 34–35, 36).
4. *Milton's Brief Epic: The Genre, Meaning, and Art of "Paradise Regained"* (Providence: Brown University Press, 1966), 341.
5. Cf. Milton, *Christian Doctrine*, ed., Maurice Kelley, trans. John Carey, in *Complete Prose Works of John Milton*, ed., Don M. Wolfe et al. (New Haven: Yale University Press, 1953–82), VI (1976), 420 (I, xvi). This edition is henceforth cited as YP.
6. *Ibid.*, 545 (I, xxviii).
7. *Milton and Modern Man* (University, Ala.: University of Alabama Press, 1968), 132, n. 5.
8. *Student's Milton*, 442 (CM, III, 4; see YP, I, 523 n. 15).
9. *Student's Milton*, 449 (CM, III, 23).
10. *Christian Doctrine*, YP, VI, 544, n. 6.
11. Louis L. Martz, *The Paradise Within* (New Haven: Yale University Press, 1966), 130.
12. *The Heavenly Muse: A Preface to Milton*, ed., Hugh MacCallum (Toronto: Toronto Press, 1972), 325 (originally published as "Theme and Pattern in *Paradise Regained, UTQ*, 25 [1956], 167–82). Cf. Warner G. Rice, "*Paradise Regained*," in *Milton: Modern Essays in Criticism*, ed., Arthur E. Barker (New York, 1965), 419: "the whole action of the poem turns upon the Devil's attempt to corrupt, and at the same time to find out the real Nature of, Christ."
13. Woodhouse, *The Heavenly Muse*, 327; Don C. Allen, *The Harmonious Vision* (Baltimore: Johns Hopkins, 1954), 111–12; Walter MacKellar, ed., *Variorum Commentary* on *Paradise*

Regained (New York: Columbia University Press, 1975), IV, 32–33, 58. Jacques Blondel is also more or less on this side; see *Paradis reconquis*, ed., Blondel (Paris: Aubier, 1955), 47–49.

14. Elizabeth M. Pope, *"Paradise Regined": The Tradition and the Poem* (rpt. ed., New York: Russell & Russell, 1962), 31.

15. Douglas Bush, *English Literature in the Earlier Seventeenth Century* 2d ed. (Oxford: Oxford University Press, 1962), 412; *John Milton* (New York: Macmillan, 1964) 184; *Complete Poetical Works*, 460; Kenneth Muir, *John Milton* (London: Longmans, 1955), 168; Edward Cleveland, "On the Identity Motive in *Paradise Regained*," *MLQ*, 16 (1955), 232–36; David Daiches, *Milton* (London: Hutchinson, 1957), 218; Arnold Stein, *Heroic Knowledge* (Minneapolis: University of Minnesota Press, 1957), 11, 37; George Williamson, *Milton and Others*, 2d ed. (Chicago: University of Chicago Press, 1970), 67, 83; Lewalski, *Milton's Brief Epic*, 134–35, 159; William B. Hunter, Jr., "The Heresies of Satan," in *Th'Upright Heart and Pure*, ed., Amadeus Fiore (Pittsburgh: Duquesne University Press, 1967), 31–32; Burton J. Weber, *Wedges and Wings: The Patterning of "Paradise Regained"* (Carbondale, Ill.: Southern Illinois University Press, 1975) 17, 91.

16. Not, as MacKellar says (*Variorum Commentary*, IV, 33), "most unequivocal."

17. John Carey, ed., with Alastair Fowler, *Poems* (London: Longmans, 1968), 1091.

18. *Ibid.*, 529.

19. MacKellar, IV, 58.

20. Joseph A. Wittreich, Jr., ed., *The Romantics on Milton* (Cleveland: Case Western Reserve University Press, 1970), 207–08.

21. YP, VI, 213 (I, v).

22. H.M. Gwatkin in *Cambridge Mediaeval History*, I, 219, quoted by Charles N. Cochrane, *Christianity and Classical Culture* (New York: Oxford Galaxy, 1957), 233. Cf. C.A. Patrides: "The teachings of Arius are terminal not only because they are theologically suspect but because they amount to a scheme which, in abrogating the felicities of human discourse, abrogates itself" ("Milton and the Arian Controversy," *Proceedings of the American Philosophical Society*, CXX, no. 4 [1976], 247). In the year in which I published, Edward W. Tayler was calling Satan "a kind of fundamentalist of the imagination...a would–be exegete lacking the power to discern anything beyond the literal sense." *Milton's Poetry* (Pittsburgh: Duquesne University Press, 1979), 82.

23. "Satan...stresses the power of the Parthians, by whom alone the power of the Messiah might be established; but he does so in part by falsifying the historical record plainly set forth by Josephus concerning the involved relationship of the Parthians to Antigonus,

Hyrcanus, and Herod, all of whom sought the throne of Judaea. Not only was their power more limited than Satan suggests, but as allies the Parthians were unreliable. Josephus, in recording the very same incidents alluded to by Satan, observed that the perfidiousness of the Parthians was notorious" (Michael Fixler, *Milton and the Kingdoms of God* [Evanston: Northwestern University Press, 1964] 264–65).

24. *Wars of the Jews*, VI, v. 4. in *Works*, trans. William Whiston (Halifax: Milner & Sowerby, 1857), 607.

25. Cf. *Christian Doctrine*, YP, VI, 334 (I, viii).

26. Henry Bettensen, ed., *Documents of the Christian* Church (New York: Oxford University Press, 1947), 52 (from Irenaeus, *Adv. haer*. I. xxvi. 1). I might add that the first translation of *Paradise Regained* avoids, by omitting, the "at least" ambiguity: "si forsitan est fas / Hunc vocitare virum, quoniam genitricis in alvo / Parte sui conclusus erat" (William Hog [Gulielmo Hogaeo], *Paraphrasis Poetica...in...Paradisum Amissum, Paradisum Recuperatum, et Samsonem Agonisten* [London, 1690], 387).

27. Harry A. Wolfson, *The Philosophy of the Church Fathers*, 3d ed. (Cambridge, Mass.: Harvard University Press, 1970), 592.

28. "Heresies of Satan," 31–32. Hunter gives *Paradise Regained* these two pages and Satan the one heresy, his provocative essay being mainly about *Paradise Lost*. He adds in regard to the temptation of classical learning that "classical philosophy was considered to be a fertile source of heresy" (32).

29. 1658 edition of *Pansebeia: or a view of all religions in the world*, 239, quoted by Malcolm M. Ross in *Poetry and Dogma* (1954; rpt. ed., New York: Octagon, 1969), 116. *Pansebeia* is one of the contemporary treatises, along with Ephraim Pagitt's *Heresiography* and Thomas Edwards' *Gangraena*, that glanced unfavorably at Milton's heresy of divorce.

30. Sonnet XVI of *A Divine Century of Spiritual Sonnets*, in *Select Poetry Chiefly Devotional of the reign of Queen Elizabeth*, ed., Edward Farr (Cambridge, 1845), I, 441, quoted (not in connection with Milton) in Ross, *Poetry and Dogma*, 71.

31. F.L. Cross, ed., *Oxford Dictionary of the Christian Church* (London: Oxford University Press, 1958), s.v. (where the date of Constantinople II is wrongly printed as "543"--and remains uncorrected in the 2nd ed. of 1974). Although all he cites of *Paradise Regained* is III, 204–05, Patrides has provided a well-documented survey of this heresy, from Clement to Kazantzakis, in "The Salvation of Satan," *JHI*, 28 (1967), 467–78. Paul Johnson quotes George Eder's *Evangelical Inquisition* of 1573 on the sect of "the Devillers (who believed the Devil would be saved on Judgment Day)" (*A History of Christianity* [New York: Atheneum,

1976], 293). I should say that I do not quarrel with the reasonableness of the following summary: "The appeal of Satan's rhetoric is not that the Son should directly redeem Satan—Satan has admitted that total redemption is impossible—but that Satan's present state should not be aggravated" (William E. McCarron, "The `persuasive Rhetoric' of *Paradise Regained*," *Milton Quarterly*, 10 [1976], 18). But take this step, and universalism, universal salvation, is next. Robert Hodge comments on *PL* VI, 857: "`timorous flock' couldn't be goats. Are there some devils who are sheep, destined to be saved at the last judgment? It would be strange if M meant this here, most unorthodox" (*Paradise Lost: Books V–VI*, gen. ed., J.B. Broadbent [Cambridge: Cambridge University Press, 1975], 127). The flock are swine, according to Mother M. Christopher Pecheux, "The Conclusion of Book VI of *Paradise Lost*," *SEL*, 3 (1963), 109–17.

32.   *Christian Doctrine*, YP, VI, 790 (II, xvi) and n. 1.

33.   Aquinas, *Summa Theologiae*, Part II, First Part, q 84, a 4, ad 5, ed., T.C. O'Brien (New York and London: McGraw, 1964), XXVI, 76–77.

34.   *Les Provinciales, or, The Mystery of Jesuitisme* (London, 1658), 58 (Letter V). On Milton's ownership of a copy see CM, XVIII, 581; J. Milton French, *The Life Records of John Milton* (New Brunswick, N.J.: Rutgers University Press, 1949–58), IV, 199; V, 129. The full sentence in the original is: "Le célèbre casuiste Basile Ponce l'a dit et le Père Bauny le cite et approuve son sentiment, que voici dans le *Traité de la Pénitence*, q. 14. 94: *On peut rechercher une occasion directement et pour elle-même*; primo et per se, *quand le bien spirituel ou temporel de nous ou de notre prochain nous y porte*" (*Oeuvres Complètes*, ed., Jacques Chevalier [Paris: Gallimard, 1954], 709). Jeremy Taylor gives many instances to which he says the apostle's rule does not apply, including "David's eating the shew-bread, and the apostles' eating corn on the Sabbath," which "served a greater need than could have been secured by superstitious or importunate abstinence" (*Ductor Dubitantium; or, The Rule of Conscience*, I, v, Rule VIII, in *Whole Works*, ed., Reginald Heber [London: Ogle, Duncan & Co., 1822], XII, 167; cf. 161).

35.   Besides entries on Busembaum (a.k.a. Busenbaum) in the usual encyclopedias, see *Biographie universelle* and *Dictionnaire de théologie catholique*. *Encyclopaedia Britannica*, 9th ed., XIII, 651, cites several Jesuits to the same effect. For a more favorable view of Busembaum see *Catholic Encyclopedia* and *New Catholic Encyclopedia*. The standard compilation is H. Denzinger, *Enchiridion Symbolorum Definitionum et Declarationum de Rebus Fidei et Morum*, of which the 28th edition issued from Freiburg in

1952. The Protestant church historian Adolf Harnack found on record in Denzinger "true knavish tricks" (*Outlines of the History of Dogma* [Boston: Beacon Press, 1957], 526).

36. The *Index* for CM, VII, 191, goes verbally astray by giving a "Jesuit" reference that is only in the English translation: Milton's Latin has *Loiolita(m)*; cf. *ibid.*, 282, 334. *Lycidas* may hold a Jesuit allusion. See "'That Two-Handed Engine' and Savonarola and the Blackfriars Fatal Vespers," in my *Poets' Riddles: Essays in Seventeenth-Century Explication* (Port Washington, N.Y.: Kennikat Press, 1975), 117-20.

37. William Riley Parker, *Milton: A Biography* (Oxford: Oxford University Press, 1968), I, 10.

38. *Student's Milton*, 738 (CM, IV, 310).

39. YP, I, 362. Mother Mary Christopher Pecheux quotes this, but does not apply it to the first temptation ("Sin in *Paradise Regained*: The Biblical Background," in *Calm of Mind*, ed., Joseph Anthony Wittreich, Jr. [Cleveland: Case Western Reserve University Press, 1971], 50).

40. MacKellar, *Variorum Commentary*, IV, 127.

41. *Grace Before Meat*, quoted ibid., 129.

42. *The Noble Voice* (New York: Holt, 1946), 139.

43. Harris F. Fletcher, *Milton's Rabbinical Readings* (Urbana, Ll.: University of Illinois Press, 1930), 186, n.; J.M. Evans, *"Paradise Lost" and the Genesis Tradition* (Oxford: Oxford University Press, 1968), 55, 65, 73, n., 101,n.

44. Abraham Cowley, n. 16 to Book I of *Davideis*, in *Poems*, ed., A.R. Waller (Cambridge: Cambridge University Press, 1905), 270.

45. *The Geneva Bible: A Facsimile of the 1560 Edition*, with an introduction by Lloyd E. Berry (Madison: University of Wisconsin Press, 1969), 2v, note d.

46. Parker, *Milton*, I, 395. On antitrinitarianism, see H. John MacLachlan, *Socinianism in Seventeenth-Century England* (Oxford: Oxford University Press, 1951); and Christopher Hill, *Milton and the English Revolution* (London: Faber & Faber, 1977), 285-96. *Time* for February 27, 1978, had a summary of current redefinitions, "New Debate over Jesus' Divinity," 44-45.

SLY MILTON:
THE MEANING LURKING IN THE CONTEXTS
OF HIS QUOTATIONS

Milton's Elegia III, on the death of Bishop Lancelot Andrewes, is extraordinarily interesting on two counts--for its echoes of Ovid and for its anticipation of Milton's English poetry. To take up the latter first, the dream vision of the bishop in Heaven looks forward to the sonnet on the "late espousèd saint" who came down from Heaven to visit the poet , her husband, in his sleep (which in turn connects with Adam's dream of Eve, VIII. 474 ff.).[1] The wife's countenance shines through a white veil, as the Bishop's does despite a white fillet encircling his head. In both cases the poet very much regrets the end of the dream. Heavenly song greets the transfigured Andrewes as it does Lycidas. For the picture of paradise the gardens of Alcinous are invoked, as they are in V. 340–41 and IX. 441. "*Lapsus praetereuntis aquae*" (22) is the forerunner of "liquid lapse of murmuring streams" (VIII. 263), as "*Flumina...argentea*" (45) is of "silver... rivers" (VIII. 437). Line 30 has, as Todd noted, resemblance to a line in what will be Milton's first English poem, "On the Death of a Fair Infant," 21: "Unhoused thy virgin soul from her fair biding-place." "King Lucifer" in the Elegy (50) is still the benign sun (not, as Thomas Warton thought, the devil), but a terrible Horatian figure, Death, knocks on the walls of princes and dispatches them with his scythe: it is a time of plague, as it will be when 'that two-handed engine" is "at the door" eleven years later.

The last half of the elegy, containing the beatific vision, is the better half, but, as Milton was to note when he similarly elevated his friend Charles Diodati at the end of "Epitaphium Damonis," Heaven is not without its "orgies" (219). Virgins like Milton and Diodati will eventually have their reward. Meanwhile one could read Ovid, and Milton did. He signalled that he did, most peculiarly, with the last line of Elegy III: "May such dreams come to me often!" Ovid had said, "May such noons come to me often!" But where and in what connection the Roman poet said it was

51

more than the early commentators could bear to specify. Warton did the first pointing out by declaring he wouldn't: "Ovid concludes one of his most exceptionable Elegies in the AMORES, which I will not point out, with such a pentameter."[2] The Reverend Henry John Todd, in his nineteenth-century variorum editions normally a faithful repeater of Warton, dispensed with this note, as did those excellent Victorian editors, Thomas Keightley and David Masson. Landor maintained a teasing vagueness: "Ovid has expressed the same wish in the same words, but the aspiration was for somewhat very dissimilar to a bishop of Winchester."[3]

So what was the "somewhat"? Walter MacKellar's 1930 edition of the Latin poems is as silent as the nineteenth-century editors. It is hardly accurate to say with Davis P. Harding that the "adaptation was first pointed out by Professor Rand,"[4] but that Harvard classicist did at last give the exact reference that three centuries of Milton's readers, by virtue of their education, wouldn't have needed. Rand, in 1922, was repeated by Bush in 1932 and Hughes in 1937.[5] Milton's last line echoes the last line of *Amores* I.v, the most lascivious of the *Amores* and the one which, as Bush observed, "contributed a good deal to Marlowe's picture of Hero naked before her lover."[6] Since Milton as an inevitably imitative Renaissance versifier borrowed many phrases, from Plautus and Virgil to Buchanan and Beza and, possibly, phrase-books, it remains to be shown that we are not in the presence here of one accidental resemblance, another patch in a crazy quilt. The connection with Ovid's little poem runs all down the line.

Ovid deftly sets his scene and hurries to his amorous conclusion all in thirteen elegiac couplets. The day was hot, the blinds let in but little light--not too much to discourage immodesty in a modest girl, the poet was alone on his bed when Corinna entered, lightly clad. To but faint resistance he stripped her, felt and admired her body. "Why go into details? All I saw was laudable, and I pressed her naked to my body. Who doesn't know the rest? When we were exhausted we both lay quiet. May such noons come to me often!"

Milton, too, in a verbally parallel line has stretched out on his bed limbs in need of refreshing. "*Ecce*" (Milton, 53; Ovid, 9)--lo and behold!--a figure appears by his bed, not a girl but a bishop,[7] in a bishop's--or blessed soul's--unisex raiment right down to the ankles. The garb of both is an important and dwelt-on point. "*Candida*"--gleaming white--(Milton, 55; Ovid, 10) is the word for both apparitions. As for Corinna, "Nowhere in her whole body was there any fault." (Curiously, Aubrey quoted the line to laud Milton!)[8] The bishop's faults have been forgiven, or he wouldn't be in Heaven. There he received embraces (61). The Freudian will find highly ambiguous the line, "Come, son, and in bliss partake of the joys of your father's kingdom" (the parental Miltons in bed!). Ovid's pair took rest after their labors; Andrewes is invited to do the same. Milton is waked up from his blissful vision by a mistress ("*pellice*")—only it happens to be Cephalus' mistress, Aurora, the dawn. (Ovid alluded to the dawn in describing the quality of light in the room.) "May such dreams come to me often!"

We progress, then, from the Columbia *Variorum Commentary's* faithful recording of three lines that are verbally parallel[9] to noticing a structural resemblance that, however odd, cannot be dismissed as coincidence. Professor Bush adds for the last line Tibullus' "May this happen to me!" (1.1.48),[10] thus giving us triple entendre, for that poet whom Ovid mourned in *Amores*, III. ix has the same context of lovers in bed.

What are we to make of all this? The latest commentator, confining his attention, as has been the custom, to the last line, calls it "a most un-Miltonic howler."[11] I don't think anything in Milton is un-Miltonic, and I shall be looking at other cases of incongruity. Meanwhile I offer, without choosing, five explanations:

(1) Milton, who was only seventeen and a slow bloomer and not yet a master of decorum, is carrying to an ingenious extreme *imitatio*, on which he was brought up, childishly, tastelessly, let the hips fall where they may. It is disheartening to consider how little change in literary education there had been since the fifth century, about which the Loeb Library editor of Sidonius comments: "The highest compliment which could be paid by one fifth-century writer to another was that he recalled one or more of the ancients. Creative work in the true sense was not fostered in the schools. The training in rhetoric had the same tendency as that given by the *grammaticus*. The study of rhetoric, though not without good points, had for centuries emphasized the importance of form rather than of matter. A straining after effect, an ostentatious and often unnatural use of words, forced antithesis, far-fetched conceits, silly paradoxes, over-elaboration and a constant sacrifice of clearness to cleverness—these were some of the features which this training too often produced."[12] Of a 16th-century imitation of Virgil that misfired (in fact the author, Aonio Paleario, was burned at the stake), John Addington Symonds perceptively remarked, "How close Milton's path lay to the worst faults in poetry, and how wonderfully he escaped, may well be calculated by the study of such verse as this."[13]

(2) Milton is amusing himself and his readers with parody. The Bishop of Winchester (object of attack in *The Reason of Church Government* sixteen years later) means nothing to him personally. Why not break up, undermine, or modify the solemnity of a conventional epicedium? Why not display the wit of a metaphysical—or should we say Chaucerian—poet? It is as if *Paradise Lost* were to become a beast fable, the squawking of Chaunticleer, Pertelote, and the Fox.[14]

(3) A colleague, Myron Taylor, suggests allegory, a sort of *Ovide Moralisé*, or Christianized. There is no lack of precedent here—King James I of Aragon at a formal assembly "rose and began a text of

Scripture"[15]--only it turned out to be a line of the *Ars Amatoria*, the same work which two centuries afterwards, 1467, a monk of Paris copied "ad laudem et gloriam Virginis Mariae."[16] Let Ovid be the superficially unlikely "golden key / That opes the palace of Eternity" (*Comus*, 13–14).

(4) If allegory is too formal a word, there is the comment that the late Gilbert Highet made on reading the first version of this article: "Milton decided very early to take over as much as he could from the best of pagan poetry and elevate it by translating it into pure Christian terms and contexts. Not merely to imitate or to parody, but to transcend." One thinks in this connection of James H. Sims' apt phrase, "Christened classicism."[17]

(5) Sexual preoccupation, or sexual frustration, will out, however deviously. (Ovid will out: he is named in verses Milton wrote days later, "*In Obitum Praesulis Eliensis*," 18.)

Explanation No. 1 may well be right, but it will encounter prejudice. It isn't very interesting, Miltonists can't be expected to like it, and it doesn't give a would-be critic much room to move around, except as he may wish to trace Milton's literary development (not that these are proper reasons for dismissal).

Explanation No. 2 (like 3 and 4) points to that development, since *Paradise Lost*, mirror of opposites, in part is--and contains--parody. Our shocks of recognition have been amply registered by now. Satan, Sin, and Death, we see, are an Unholy Trinity, a more dynamic *rappresentazione* than Dante's tri-faced monster. Pandemonium parodies the Pantheon in Rome and possibly St. Peter's. "Secret conclave sat" (I. 795) directs our thoughts to locked-up cardinals electing a Pope. The Paradise of Fools parodies going on pilgrimage and superstitious formulae for salvation. The deluded ones are sent flying "o'er the backside of the world" (III, 494). Book VI satirizes war, and epic descriptions of it, "long and tedious havoc...In battles feigned" (XI. 30–31). Satan's entering the body of a serpent parodies the Incarnation, the kenosis. His words at IX. 713–14 pervert I Cor. 15.53. "There is...in *Paradise Lost*, not only a respect for the great cultural traditions of the past, but also a kind of witty devaluation of them, or inversion of them." *Paradise Lost*, besides being the culmination of epic, is anti-epic, "a kind of joke against the epic."[18] Milton has his cake and eats it too. A cunning example that Addison paused over is the odd reminiscence of the most sensual passage in *The Iliad* (XIV. 292–353). Fallen lustful Adam ogles Eve as if she were Hera equipped with Aphrodite's girdle ("zone of Venus," *Paradise Regained*, II. 214), and he says to her what Zeus said on that deceitful occasion. The hyacinth helped make up the flowery bed of both couples, both couplers. This is a two-way devaluation, and approximately as miscellaneous a mixture of pagan and divine as tossing Corinna and the Bishop of Winchester into the same bed: yet there sounds withal a fond ("loving" *and* "foolish") and deliberate regret for past pleasures, humanistic and carnal, and it has "contagious fire" (IX. 1036). "But come, so well refreshed, now let us play" (IX. 1027) translates *Iliad* XIV. 314. But it also translates *Iliad* III. 441, Paris to Helen, and *Odyssey* VIII. 292, Ares to Aphrodite on taking advantage of her husband's absence. Thus the illicit is added to the main recollection (Zeus and Hera, however much they deceived each other, were legal partners), and the third reminiscence adds the shame and punishment of being caught, as guilty Adam and Eve are caught by God.[19]

On explanation No. 5, the sexual, which is almost too interesting, I can truly say, I could write a book.[20] One is led to seek out other hidden sexual allusions. A case that Rand noticed but that Hughes left out of his omnibus edition of 1957[21] and the classics–conscious John Carey doesn't have either is Elegia V, "On the Coming of Spring," 8. Milton is rejoicing in the seasonal return of his powers ("*vires*") as a poet. Inspiration has come and "now demands some work for itself." This remembers *Amores* III. vii. 68, a poem about impotence. At the wrong time, when it's too late, the poet's "*membra*" "now demand work." In the previous line Ovid had "*vigent*"; Milton has "*vigescit*." Milton's piece, this time, is openly erotic, but only the fit (or properly briefed) reader will catch the sly equation between poetic inspiration and male potency.

I had a colleague who committed, to quote Joyce, "Hearasay in paradox lust" (*Finnegans Wake*, 263). He declared that "the dirtiest line in Milton" is IV. 311. He said this before B.A. Wright published a note citing Ovid (*Notes and Queries*, n.s. 5 [1958]. 341). The *context* of "And sweet reluctant amorous delay" is definitely not that of sexual union in the bower, to say nothing of *carezza*. We are just being introduced to the couple. What Eve "yielded" was "Subjection." But, after all, "subjection" means "placed underneath" (the pun of "At a Vacation Exercise," 74–80), and Ovid allows us to peep into Milton's associations, which are anticipatory of the bower. *Ars Amatoria*, II. 717 ff., like modern manuals, advises that Venus is not to be hurried, that delay is sweet. The Roman's recommendation was to touch the lady in the right places. "Believe me, the pleasure of love is not to be hurried, but to be elicited gradually with prolonged delay." Milton's "reluctant" has the etymological indication of a certain amount of struggling, reinforcing the gradualness of "Yielded with coy submission." And these are the lines about which the modest Landor exclaimed, "I would rather have written these two lines than all the poetry that has been written since Milton's time in all the regions of the earth'!"[22] It is no accident that next comes the "mysterious parts" lecture.

Milton does not blush for "those mysterious parts": on the contrary he gives a good deal of attention to them. Nor did he shrink from admitting in public his early fondness for "the smooth Elegiack Poets"–– Ovid, Tibullius, Propertius, not just for their style but "for their matter which what it is, there be few who know not, I was so allur'd to read, that no recreation came to me better welcome" (*Works*, III, 302). He seems to be saying he was *homme moyen sensuel,* and "there be few who" are not. Scott Elledge puts no fine point upon it: "he had a strongly sensual nature."[23]

In any case Comus had a strongly sensual nature, and armed with the knowledge that Milton was interested in *Ars Amatoria*, II. 717 ff., I think I find it lurking behind a certain rather problematic passage. The *Mask* has long been looked at lately in ways calculated to turn crimson the faces of Warton, Todd, and Landor. It has been suggested that it expressed the Bridgewater "family's need to see its last unmarried daughter enact sexual virtue and restraint," since Lady Alice Egerton's cousin Elizabeth had been turned into a "whore" at the age of twelve and the Earl of Castlehaven beheaded in May 1631 for his part in the criminal proceedings, which also included rape and sodomy.[24] We have been told that Comus' wand is "phallic."[25] Comus' "marble venomed seat" which holds the Lady immobilized is "Smeared with gums of glutinous heat" (917). Is that, it has been asked and affirmed in *Milton Quarterly*, a reference to semen, with a pun on *gluteus*, buttocks?[26]

Let us, therefore, give "low-thoughted care" (6) to what is evidently sexual advice from Comus by way of Ovid:

> List, lady, be not coy, and be not cozened
> With that same vaunted name Virginity;
> Beauty is Nature's coin, must not be hoarded,
> But must be current, and the good thereof
> Consists in mutual and partaken bliss,
> Unsavory in th'enjoyment of itself.

"Mutual and partaken bliss"--mutual and simultaneous orgasm? "Unsavory in th'enjoyment of itself"--a criticism of the practice of masturbation?[27] This passage, which should bring a blush to any Lady's cheeks, was in fact dropped at the original performance. The *Variorum Commentary* offers the following suggestive gloss and quotation on "mutual": "The common meaning is perhaps coloured by a meaning now obsolete, `intimate,' as in `The stealth of our most mutual entertainment / With character too gross is writ on Juliet' (Shakespeare, *Meas.* I.2.158-9)"[28] (referring to Juliet's being "with child" [next line] of Claudio). Young Milton, making up by reading what he lacked in experience, has drawn, not for the last time, on a favorite portion of *Ars Amatoria*. The Roman handbook gave out the information that neither partner of the bed should get ahead of the other. "Hurry to your goal together. That is full bliss *(plena voluptas)* when the man and woman lie equally conquered" (II. 727-28).

Sometimes Milton has censored his sources. The Lady, in her reply, can be detailed, in all decency, only about gluttony:

...swinish gluttony
Ne'er looks to Heav'n amidst his gorgeous feast,
But with besotted base ingratitude
Crams, and blasphemes his Feeder.   (776–79)

Editors fail to note the pun in "gorgeous." Gorging, eating and drinking, is Comus' prelude to copulation, and the Lady's subsequent reference to "Chastity" (782) shows her understanding of what he has in mind. The source of the quoted lines, as pointed to by Paul Shorey and John Carey, supplies the missing word. Plato's *Republic* (586A) alludes to "those who have no experience of wisdom and virtue...but with eyes ever bent upon the earth and heads bowed down over their tables they feast like cattle, grazing and copulating."[29] Having gone from cattle to swine (as the Circe myth dictated), Milton returns to cattle in *The Doctrine and Discipline of Divorce*, where he scorns "the meer motion of carnall lust" as the principal motivation in marriage and the dissolution of marriage: "God does not principally take care for such cattell" (*Works*, III, 396). Raphael also singles out for their sexual activity "cattle" (VIII, 582).

Whenever Martin Bucer, in his remarks on divorce, gets cattle-like, or too restrictive, Milton simply refuses to translate him. Witness the following notes and translations by Arnold Williams in the Yale Milton:

Milton omits..."after the nuptial festivities have been celebrated, and thus plenty of carnal intercourse enjoyed, then it were seasonable enough for their nuptial pact to take full firmness."

Milton omits..."in which it is said, it is better to marry than to burn, and younger widows are commanded to marry."

Milton omits a passage...citing Ambrose to the effect that a man putting away his wife for adultery should remain unmarried, but is not compelled.

Milton omits three paragraphs...in which Bucer makes the point that marriage consists essentially in continuous cohabitation, except for special cause and for short periods.

Milton omits..."from which the Lord concluded in the Gospel that it behooves spouses whom the Lord has joined in marriage to be not two, but one flesh."

Milton omits a passage... developing the danger of fornication to a man compelled to live with an intolerable wife.[30]

After being so revealingly selective Milton may well proclaim "that my mother bore me a speaker of what God made mine own, and not a translator" (*Works*, IV, 60). He admits leaving out Bucer's Chapters XXXII–IV dealing with adultery, with which along with impotence, this lofty-minded reformer found canon law too much concerned: "...he who affirms adultery to be the highest breach, affirms the bed to be the highest of mariage, which is in truth a grosse and borish opinion, how common soever" (*Works*, III, 415).

Another case of purifying a source is the "Teian Muse" (Anacreon) parallel between Elegia VI. 21–22 and Ovid's *Tristia*, II. 263–64. Here I must agree with Harding that "Milton's Anacreon sings innocently of wine and roses; he imparts no instructions on the best methods of combining wine with Venus."[31] Similarly, in inserting in his Commonplace Book a note from the French historian Thuanus about the entry into bigamy––after conference with his pastors––of Landgrave Philip of Hesse, Milton (who after his first wife deserted him entertained a bigamous "design of Marrying one of Dr. *Davis's* Daughters"[32]) did not choose to record what Thuanus tells of that Protestant prince's inexhaustible capacity for venery and abnormal anatomical endowment.[33] (One might add in passing that discussions of whether Adam could or should have married after Eve was lost would sound more substantial if they condescended to look at Milton's own practice and theory. Eve, like Mary Powell Milton, was worried over Lilith or Miss Davis or whatever a second wife's name would be––IX. 828 ff. Eve, not having read the divorce tracts, doesn't know that an Adam who resisted the forbidden fruit might not even have waited for her to die before remarrying.)

Milton, in describing the couple as they engorge, uses an expression that conceivably was prompted by another favorite poet, Chaucer:

> They swim in mirth, and fancy that they feel
> Divinity within them breeding wings
> Wherewith to scorn the earth.   (IX. 1009–11)

"They swim in mirth": this figurative use of "swim" is covered under––in fact quoted under––*OED* 9b, but I wonder if there is a tincture of the literal that foreshadows a play on words later in the poem. If so, the riddle is, what swims and has wings? Not an angel, not particularly a god, but a duck:

> Thanne shaltou swymme as myrie, I undertake,
> As dooth the white doke after hire drake.
> Thanne wol I clepe, `How, Alison! how, John!
> Be myrie, for the flood wol passe anon.'
> And thou wolt seyn, `Hayl, maister Nicholay!
> Good morwe, I see thee wel, for it is day.'
> And thanne shul we be lordes al oure lyf
> Of al the world, as Noe and his wyf.
>   ("The Miller's Tale," 3575–82)

In a triangular situation the old Nick has been sucesssfully deceptive; so has the clerk Nicholas. And the proper relation and hierarchy between man and wife has been disrupted. (Milton in his Commonplace Book, XVIII, 151, had recorded his interest in those parts of Chaucer that showed "the discommodities of mariage": he limited mention to "The Merchant's Tale" and "The Wife of Bath's Prologue.") John the carpenter thinks he is leading his white duck, and he should be, but she is leading—and misleading—him. The unhappy couples will discover they cannot "scorn the earth," "be lordes...Of al the world." Noah's flood comes afterward, of course, in the epic, but already Nature "some drops / Wept at completing of the mortal sin" (IX. 1002–03), and, as if to annotate his earlier expression, the poet returns to it punningly: "now swim in joy / (Erelong to swim at large)" (XI. 625–26). Thus Milton gets around to giving us in earnest what Chaucer had in jest.[34]

Leo Spitzer wrote a much–reprinted article subtitled "Sources versus Meaning."[35] We, however, have been reviewing instances where sources contribute to meaning. A missing element is added. Sometimes that element can be inferred, as with the Lady's reply, and only awaits confirmation. To give another instance, one may be surprised that Sin, serpentine in her lower half, doesn't have serpent offspring. Besides the biological consistency—if that may be expected of monsters—a brood of vipers would take us full "voluminous" (II. 652) circle to the guise, both voluntary and compelled, of Sin's creator and lover. But Milton, with Scylla—and also Hesiod's Echidna—in mind, gives us hell–hounds. His "substitution of Scylla's dogs for the viper's brood may involve a Latin pun. In describing the behaviour of vipers, Isidore and other commentators had referred to the young serpents as *catuli*. In its broadest sense, this term could comprehend the young of any animal, but it normally referred specifically to young dogs.[36] In any case there are vipers in the background, a missing element that slithers forward upon consideration of the following:

(1) Sir Thomas Browne (to choose one among scores of learned authorities) recorded of vipers, "For the young one supposed to break through the belly of the Dam, will upon any fright for protection run into it; for then the old one receives them in at her mouth, which way the fright being past, they will return again, which is a peculiar way of refuge."[37] Milton, thinking more of Scylla, details a still more "peculiar way of refuge," the womb.

(2) As for gnawing the mother serpent's vitals, in unnatural natural history, dogs don't behave that way, but vipers do. Browne recorded that tradition too, and Milton signalled as much in *Of Reformation* with the figure of "that *Viper* of *Sedition*, that for these Fourscore Yeares hath been breeding to eat through the entrals of our *Peace*" (*Works*, III, 77). So, in a complicated situation, the poet has his hounds and eats his snake too, and what we thought should be there *is* there, like a sunken metaphor.

To leave behind at last sex and phallic symbols, this exploration of Milton's psychology as a writer has other matters to consider, such as the sestet of the sonnet "How soon hath Time," which *sounds* modestly patient:

> Yet be it less or more, or soon or slow,
> > It shall be still in strictest measure ev'n
> > To that same lot, however mean or high,
>
> Toward which Time leads me, and the will of Heav'n;
> > All is, if I have grace to use it so,
> > As ever in my great Task-Master's eye.

Pindar has been taken as a source: "But whatsoever excellence Lord Destiny assigned me, well I know that the lapse of time will bring it to its appointed perfection."[38] Do we learn more about Milton's attitude by looking at the immediately preceding lines in Pindar? "We shall yet be deemed to come forth in the light of day far stronger than our foes, while another, with envious glance, broodeth in darkness over some fruitless purpose that falleth to the ground." Those "more timely-happy spirits" (8), they will find, will they not, that the race is not always to the swift. The time will come when Milton will be envied.

This called for mixed feelings, however. Like a superstitious ancient, he worried about being envied, even as he was not optimistic about the generality of his audience. In his Commonplace Book he gloomily noted, "Since men generally envy where they ought to praise, there is no reason to expect much from human commendation" (*Works*, XVIII, 161). Even the *Areopagitica* contains an *absit invidia* formula: "I might say, if without envy" (*Works*, IV, 330). The problem of envy he kept returning to throughout his works.[39] This prickly concern--of who will be hostile--underlies three direct quotations--three epigraphs on title pages--with which we can more firmly conclude, out in the clear from possible arguments about sources.

The first was on the title page of the *Mask* that Henry Lawes had printed without the author's name in 1637. Of all the poems from which to choose a motto, this was most unfortunate, being Virgil's homosexual Eclogue II in which the shepherd Corydon woos Alexis. As Byron said, "But Virgil's songs are pure, except that horrid one / Beginning with 'Formosum Pastor Corydon'" (*Don Juan*, I. xlii). I make nothing of this,[40] but I do make something of whither the quoted lines (58–59) are tending: "Alas, what have I wished on my miserable self, for my own loss, [letting] the south wind in on my flowers." The quotation breaks off without completing the sentence and the line. What Virgil has is: "and the wild boars on my clear springs." We understand why Milton stopped quoting: he could hardly be labelling in public his potential readers as boars, muddying up his clear springs. I am convinced, however, that that was part of his thought, not only from the context, not only from the future irate sonnets (XI and XII) about "casting pearl to hogs," but from two "boar" passages in his prose. The first, I must admit, comes as part of the prayer to the Trinity in *Of Reformation*: "these wilde *Boares* that have broke into thy *Vineyard*, and left the print of thir polluting hoofs on the Soules of thy Servants" (*Works*, III, 76). The other passage is down to earth. Milton is dealing in *Colasterion* with an unfit reader of his *Doctrine and Discipline of Divorce*: "Hee passes to the third Argument, like a Boar in a Vinyard, doing nought els, but still as he goes, champing and chewing over, what I could mean..." (*Works*, IV, 261).

The next quotation appears in Greek and English on the title page of *Areopagitica*. Milton renders into blank verse *The Suppliants* of Euripides, 438–41:

> This is true Liberty when free born men
> Having to advise the public may speak free,
> Which he who can, and will, deserv's high praise,
> Who neither can nor will, may hold his peace;
> What can be juster in a State then this?

We nod our heads in easy agreement; this all seems truistic enough now. But read on in the original, 442 ff.: "Again, where the people are absolute rulers of the land, they rejoice in having a reserve of youthful citizens, while a king counts this as a hostile element, and strives to slay the leading men, all such as he deems discreet, for he feareth for his power."[41] The word to the wise is that in November 1644, when most of his countrymen were still hoping for a compromise with the king, the future defender of tyrannicide has given up on Charles and feels personally threatened by him and sees no hope but in a republic. There is evidence that at thirty–five Milton still regarded himself as in the class of the "youthful,"[42] and he was certainly out to establish himself as "discreet," the corrector of Parliamentary error. Unless one had a martyr complex like John Lilburne the Leveller it would have been the height of folly to come out into the open with the above sentiments, part of Theseus' praise of the Athenian democracy. They would have incurred the swift punishment that the unlicensed divorce tract did not. Englishmen were fighting their king to preserve him and the kingdom and the kingship: a distinction was drawn between Charles Stuart the man and Charles I, the duly constituted monarch who had been led astray by evil counsels and evil counsellors. There was a good chance that the Parliamentarians would kill their king in battle; what they would not tolerate was criticism of him beyond very narrow limits. Indeed who can be found as thinking the unthinkable for several years to come? Consider an episode about half a year later, in 1645: "Parliament, which had nourished the rebellion, vainly strove to restrain its effects. Few in the commons were not shocked when *Mercurius Britanicus* [old misspelling] published an advertisement for a wanted man named Charles, a traitor and a runagate, who might be recognised by a stammer and an inability to speak the truth. The French envoy protested. The House of Lords took action, brought home the offensive paragraph to its authors and had them shut up in prison. They were two officers of the New Model Army, Mervyn Audley and Robert White."[43] The quotation on the title page of *Areopagitica* teeters on the brink of treason. It does not go over. But a new bite is given, by way of "his favourite dramatist,"[44] to Gooch's old summation of Milton "as the chief of those whom Hobbes describes as having in their youth read the books `written by famous men of the ancient Grecian and Roman Commonwealths, concerning their polity and their great actions, in which the popular government was extolled by the glorious name of Liberty and Monarchy disgraced by the name of tyranny, and who thereby became in love with their forms of government.'"[45] At the same time it must be understood, from what we know of the author, that the position being covertly conveyed is less pro–"popular government" than anti–tyranny. "The kind of parliament he conceived as standing at the center of power in the state was not that called for three years later in the Levellers' *Agreement of the People* but an Areopagus, a great council of worthies, hearkening at all times to instruction and admonition from those who had learned from the best authors and the Word of God...."[46] In fact we can find him, c. 1647, in the midst of the tumults around him, giving notice that "libertie hath a sharp and double edge fitt onelie to be handl'd by just and vertuous men."[47]

Apropos of that reference to "men," we should, before going on to another motto, glance at a case where Milton's convictions put him in a bind. In *A Brief History of Moscovia* he has to tell of an anti–tyranny act by a woman, Sophia, who delivered "her Husband, and his Country" from the "Yoke" of the Tartars (*Works*, X, 352). "Yoke" is the word in his source in Richard Hakluyt's *Principal Navigations* (Glasgow: Hakluyt Society, 1903, II, 189–90, quoted by Robert R. Cawley, *Milton's Literary Craftmanship* [1941; rpt. New York: Gordian Press, 1965], 8), and he has every reason to pass it on. But he finds too complimentary the initial description of Sophia in his source: "This Sophia being a woman of a princely and aspiring mind." A princely woman? It was Milton's conviction that the aspiring minds of women had caused much too much trouble ever since Eve (see reference at note 7). He changes to, "This Princess of a haughty mind."

Our third motto is the ambiguous one of the 1645 *Poems*. It, as with *Comus*, is taken from an eclogue of Virgil (VII. 27–28): "Bind my brow with baccar, lest an evil tongue harm the poet to be." This is within Milton's pattern of exhibiting anxiety. The words come from Thyrsis, the loser in a poetical competition between him and Corydon. Milton called himself Thyrsis in "Epitaphium Damonis" (then thinking, no doubt, of the Thyrsis of Theocritus, I). Another good singer he named Thyrsis in *Comus*. That the Virgilian Thyrsis doesn't receive the guerdon seems quite arbitrary, but then so did the death of Lycidas. Meanwhile evil is to be avoided, and by magic means if available. Servius Grammaticus[48] explains that baccar is a plant used to avert enchantment. Thus it links up with Homer's moly (mentioned twice in Milton's volume) and Milton's own haemony. Decking a poet's brow with ivy sets in motion a need for protection, as the immediately preceding lines in the eclogue indicated: "Shepherds, inhabitants of Arcady [*Arcades*, another cross allusion], deck the growing poet with ivy, that the spleen of Codrus may burst with envy." Such an outcome is simultaneously desirable--because it means accomplishment is recognized--and undesirable, for the "evil tongue" can do harm, and the evil eye, "the twisted eye of envy with goatish leer" ("Ad Patrem," 106, a twisting from Ecl. III. 8, as the editors note). Will Milton's poetical blossoms be nipped in the bud at this inauspicious time, a time of civil war and chiding? The collection contained Sonnet VIII, "On his door when the city expected an assault," the tone of which has been disputed, whether serious or jocular, but again we have the idea of an amulet, magic like the magic of virginity or a supernatural plant. The edition of 1645 also included an envy ("*invidia*") safeguard at the beginning of the Latin section of the volume, preceding the "*testimonic*," from the poetasters of Italy. Milton asserts he is "doing all in his power to remove from himself the envy of excessive praise." It would, I should think, have been in his power to drop the *testimonia*, but he still wants his cake. Well, maybe baccar will help. Years later, another world later, the "evil tongue" returned with a vengeance, multiplied: "fall'n on evil days, / On evil days though fall'n, and evil tongues" (VII. 25–26). Such are the uncanny connections, forward and backward in time.

If we remain puzzled that from underneath the white robe of the Bishop of Winchester gleams the white skin of Corinna, what are we to say of Jesus as a farmer? The surprise is less, but it is there. It is no callow Milton that gives us this, but the author of *Paradise Regained*. The opening lines accomplish something the commentators don't pause over:[49] they ring in a parody on the sacred and central Miltonic (and Pauline) concept "obedience" (4). In the verses being imitated here that prefaced the *Aeneid* in Renaissance editions Virgil, referring to his *Georgics*, observed, "I forced the nearby fields to obey the farmer, however hungry." Jesus, like a pioneer with "gard'ning tools" (*Paradise Lost*, IX, 391), "Eden raised in the waste wilderness" (*Paradise Regained*, I. 7). Jesus by obeying God causes the fields to obey Jesus. From obedient fields to obedient Jesus is a giant step from rhetoric to logic--or ought we to say Logos? It stands as only one of the surprises in a poet who did not hesitate "to compare / Small things with greatest" (*Paradise Regained*, IV. 563–64). Perhaps it is a mark of the author's maturity, as well as of the greater gravity of the poem, that the latent reference does not smack of shocking incongruity. Indeed, the more we contemplate it the more appropriate it seems. A different exponential power (Virgil, Ovid) is raising a different figure (Jesus, the Bishop of Winchester). "Raised" gives us the carpenter's son at work. (On the divine side of his nature he "raised us from the dust and placed us here"--*Paradise Lost*, IV. 416--and will raise again.) Turning "waste wilderness" into Eden--"I am the true vine, and my Father is the husbandman" (John 15.1)--is done by the teller of parables that take their imagery and reference from husbandry: "Wherefore by their fruits ye shall know them" (Mat. 7.20); "The harvest truly is plenteous, but the laborers are few" (Mat. 9.37); "A sower went out to sow his seed" (Luke 8.5); "The kingdom of heaven is like to a grain of mustard seed" (Mat. 13.31). Jesus is like a farmer. "He that soweth the good seed is the Son of man" (Mat. 13.37).[50] Milton's only new point is, "He that hath ears to hear, let him hear" (Mat. 11.15; Mark 4.9; Luke 8.8; 14.35) the Renaissance Virgil's reference to the *Georgics*, encompassing a figure of obedience.

Thirty-five years ago when I published a note with the title "Milton Remembers *The Praise of Folly*" (*PMLA*, 71 [1956], 840), I didn't know that I had stumbled upon one piece in a pattern, other pieces of which are sorted out here, with still more, in all likelihood, yet to be noticed. It did seem that we were vouchsafed a glimpse of Milton's frame of mind, or mood, a few weeks before he gave up bachelorhood. I called him "remarkably personal" when, in the fourth sentence of *An Apology for Smectymnuus*, he alluded to "the wearisome labours and studious watchings, wherein I have spent and tir'd out almost a whole youth" (*Works*, 3, 282). He was more or less quoting Erasmus,[51] but, as in translating Bucer, he censored, he left something significant out. What he left out was the conclusion that the scholar who grinds away his youth has kept himself "for the rest of his life from tasting a bit of pleasure" ("*tantillum voluptatis*"). Milton was determined that this wouldn't happen to him. He went to Forest Hill and returned with a bride half his age. The "bit of pleasure" was -- O voice of Folly!--Mary Powell Milton, that mixed blessing, that precious bane.

To sum up, pursuing Milton's sources and the contexts of his quotations (as well as his borrowings from himself)[52] results, in a number of instances, in speculative bounty: his submerged thoughts or associations, or a message about which, at least at the moment he wrote, he was not explicit.[53] We are to read around the lines, "by indirections find directions out." As a reader (of Scripture), he himself advised "examination...of what comes before and after the passage in question" (Yale *Prose*, 6, 582). The search is exhilarating, the catch controversial: some, perhaps, will say it isn't there at all.

NOTES

1. The verbal links between Son. XXIII and the epic are traced in my *Yet Once More: Verbal and Psychological Pattern in Milton* (1953; rpt. New York: AMS Press, 1969), 15–17. In the present work I quote Milton's poetry from Douglas Bush, ed., *Complete Poetical Works* (Boston: Houghton, 1965). My text for the prose comes from the *Works*, ed. F.A. Patterson and others, 18 vols. (New York: Columbia University Press, 1931–38). Mine are the translations––I keep them literal––from the Latin of Milton, Ovid, Virgil and Erasmus (and the bit of Sallust and Lucan in note 53).

2. T. Wharton, ed., *Poems upon Several Occasions*, 2nd ed. (London, 1791), 439.

3. Walter Savage Landor, *Imaginary Conversations*, "Southey and Landor," Second Conversation, in *Works* (London: Moxon, 1846), 2, 171.

4. Harding, *Milton and the Renaissance Ovid* (Urbana: University of Illinois Press, 1946), 47.

5. E.K. Rand, "Milton in Rustication," *Studies in Philology*, 19 (1922), 133; Bush, *Mythology and the Renaissance Tradition in English poetry* (Minneapolis: University of Minnesota Press, 1932), 251; Merritt Y. Hughes, ed., *"Paradise Regained," the Minor Poems, and "Samson Agonistes"* (New York: Doubleday, 1937), 43.

6. Bush, *Mythology and the Renaissance Tradition*, 251.

7. For associations to come see the "Women and Bishops" chapter in Le Comte, *Yet Once More*, 123–41.

8. "'In toto nusquam corpore menda fuit.' Ovid." *The Early Lives of Milton*, ed., Helen Darbishire (London: Constable, 1932), 4. Darbishire does not locate the quotation; worse, some later editors omit it: Oliver Lawson Dick, *Aubrey's Brief Lives* (Ann Arbor: University of Michigan Press, 1957), 201; C.A. Patrides (whose text is based on Dick), ed., John Milton, *Selected Prose* (Harmondsworth: Penguin, 1974), 372. Also lacking the tag, but without Dick's claims as a reliable transcriber, are John Collier's edition, *The Scandal and Credulities of John Aubrey* (London: Peter Davies, 1931), 100–05, and Anthony Powell's *Brief Lives* (London: Cresset Press, 1949), 70. If Aubrey's linking of Milton and Corinna was conscious, it is less odd considering that on his first leaf (Darbishire, 3) this biographer noted that the young Milton "was so faire' that at Cambridge he was called "the Lady of" Christ's College. (Confirmed by Milton, Prolusio VI, *Works*, 12, 240.) On the history of the name, see my "Herrick's Corinna," *Names*, 33 (1985), 292–95, with now this additional observation that "Corinna" is still a character in novels: Italo Calvino's *Se una*

notte d'inverno un viaggiatore, 1979; Cynthia Ozick's *The Cannibal Galaxy*, 1983.

9. Notes at ll. 35, 53–55, 68 (and cf. p. 14) in Bush, ed., *Variorum Commentary, The Latin and Greek Poems* (New York: Columbia University Press, 1970).

10. *Ibid.*, 14; ed., *Complete Poetical Works*, 19.

11. Ralph W. Condee, *Structure in Milton's Poetry: From the Foundation to the Pinnacles* (University Park: Pennsylvania State University Press, 1974), 183, n. 20.

12. W.B. Anderson, ed., Sidonius, *Poems and Letters* (London: Heinemann, 1936), I, xxxv.

13. Symonds, *Renaissance in Italy* (New York: Modern Library, n.d.), I, 560, n. 79. Besides Milton's *imitatio* as detailed in Bush's *Variorum Commentary*, Fred J. Nichols furnishes a wide–ranging survey of the Renaissance practice as editor and translator of *An Anthology of Neo–Latin Poetry* (New Haven: Yale University Press, 1979), 14 ff., with comprehensive bibliographies 653 ff.

14. "The Nun's Priest's Tale" and *Paradise Lost* are seriously joined by John E. Seaman, *The Moral Paradox of "Paradise Lost"* (The Hague: Mouton, 1971), 109–110.

15. Rand, *Ovid and His Influence* (New York: Longmans, Green, 1925), 136.

16. Clyde B. Cooper, *Some Elizabethan Opinions of the Poetry and Character of Ovid* (Menasha, Wisconsin: Collegiate Press, 1914), 11.

17. Sims, "Cristened Classicism in *Paradise Lost* and *The Lusiads*," *Comparative Literature*, 24 (1972), 338–56. The most recent discussion is by John M. Paskus, *Not Less but More Heroic: Milton's Classical and Christian Worlds* (New York: Vantage Press, 1978).

18. T.J.B. Spencer, *"Paradise Lost*:The Anti–Epic," in *Approaches to "Paradise Lost,"* ed., Patrides (London: Edward Arnold, 1968), 89, 93. See, further, Bush, "Ironic and Ambiguous Allusion in *Paradise Lost*," *Journal of English and Germanic Philology*, 60 (1961), 631–40; James Black, "The Return to Pandemonium: Interlude and Antimasque in *Paradise Lost*," *Wascana Review*, 9 (1974), 139–98; B. Rajan, "The Cunning Resemblance," *Milton Studies*, 7 (1975), 29–48. The sexual thrust at the concoctions of the Church Fathers is most daring: "The Devil, Sin, and Death are thus a monstrous parody of the Holy Trinity, the *circuminsessio* (mutual dwelling) of the three Persons of the Trinity disgustingly mirrored by this mutual incest (2.681–870)." Jeffrey Burton Russell, *Mephistopheles: The Devil in the Modern World* (Ithaca: Cornell University Press, 1986), 116. I am reminded of T.S. Eliot's characterization of poetry as "a superior amusement," which may

be that critic's best remark on Milton, though it does not occur in his essays on Milton but in his 1928 Preface to *The Sacred Wood* (New York: Barnes and Noble, 1950), viii. Long before Huizinga's *Homo Ludens*, Goethe called *Faust* "this very serious jest." Thomas Mann in 1953 picked up the phrase as "a good definition of art, of all art." "The Making of *The Magic Mountain*," in the Vintage Books ed. of the novel (New York, 1959), 721. It should be remarked that parody in *Paradise Lost*, when not literary (and even when literary it serves to put paganism in a dim light), is part of the divine comedy of permissive evil. God smiles in His mysterious way: "And smiling to his only Son thus said:" V. 718. St. Augustine comes up with a startlingly literary apology for God's ways in his discussion, *The City of God*, XI. 18, of "the beauty of the universe, which becomes, by God's ordinance, more brilliant by the opposition of contraries": "For God would never have created any, I do not say angel, but even man, whose future wickedness He foreknew, unless He had equally known to what uses in behalf of the good He could turn him, thus embellishing the course of the ages, as it were an exquisite poem set off with antitheses." Quoted by Desmond M. Hamlet, "Recalcitrance, Damnation, and the Justice of God in *Paradise Lost*," *Milton Studies*, 8 (1975), 283, in the Marcus Dods translation. The 1610 John Healey translation (*The City of God*, 3 vols. [London: Dent, 1903], II, 197--book reclassified as X. 18) ends the sentence, "so making the world's course, like a fair poem, more gracious by antithetic figures." The original reads: "*tamquam pulcherrimum carmen etiam ex quibusdam quasi antithetis honestaret.*" "Gracious" looks forward to Jesus' pun, "O Father, gracious was that word" III. 144. There are fascinating interchanges. If God is a clever poet (shall we say a metaphysical poet?) who favors *antitheta* or, in Healey's quaint Englishing, "contra-posites," Milton is what John T. Shawcross calls "The Rhetor as Creator in *Paradise Lost*" (*Milton Studies*, 8 [1975], 209-19). For theory see Eugenio Donato, "Tesauro's Poetics: Through the Looking Glass," *Modern Language Notes*, 78 (1963), 15-30. Milton "explicitly compares his poetic creation to the birth of the cosmos at the outset of his poem." Regina M. Schwartz, *Remembering and Repeating: Biblical Creation in "Paradise Lost"* (Cambridge: Cambridge University Press, 1988), 60. According to Ernst Robert Curtius, "the poet with cosmogonic powers" is a conception that the ancients lacked, though I should think that the very etymology of "poet" as "maker" would have proved suggestive, and it should be noted that Cicero, *Tusculan Disputations* I. 25-26, just before speaking of the poet, compares Archimedes' globe to the work of a demiurge. Curtius says it comes in with Macrobius' analysis of Virgil. See *European Literature and the Latin Middle Ages*, trans. Willard R. Trask (1953; rpt. Princeton: Bollingen, 1973), "Imitation and Creation," 397 ff., and the Excursuses, "Jest and Earnest in Medieval Literature," 417 ff., "Macrobius," 443 ff., and "God as Maker," 544 ff. Curtius does not mention Coleridge's description (in Ch. XIV of *Biographia Literaria* [ed. J.C. Metcalf, New York: Macmillan, 1926, 197]) of the poetic Imagination as "that synthetic and magical power" which "reveals itself in the balance or reconcilement of opposite or discordant qualities." For a provocative analysis of some similes see Melissa C. Wanamaker, *Discordia Concors: The Wit of Metaphysical Poetry* (Port Washington, N.Y.: Kennikat, 1975), Ch. VI, "John Milton: Opposites and Multiplicity Resolved," 98–124. Apropos of Nicolas of Cusa, famous for his *coincidentia oppositorum*, William Kerrigan and Gorden Braden remark: "it is immediately obvious why imagination, as the maker of what is not, should be like the creator, or in demonic terms, God's competitor. For Nicolas, however, imagination is unmistakably analogous to Christ, union of disproportionate realms." *The Idea of the Renaissance* (Baltimore: Johns Hopkins University Press, 1989), 95. God's writing is history. "It should be obvious that God in shaping history took on the role of the late medieval and Renaissance poet, writing an allegory of things, people, and events." Edward W. Tayler, *Milton's Poetry: Its Development in Time* (Pittsburgh: Duquesne University Press, 1979), 88. A (Presbyterian) clergyman editor who states flatly, by way of objecting to the Paradise of Fools, "Ludicrous sentiments are unnatural in an epic poem," is forgetting the idea of the Devil as the ape of God (*simia Dei*) and is failing to remember, in any detail, *The Iliad* and *The Odyssey*. Rev. James Robert Boyd, ed., *Paradise Lost* (New York: Baker and Scribner, 1850), 137. (One need not have read Samuel Butler's overfacetious *The Humour of Homer* of 1892 or 237 ff. of C.M. Bowra, *Tradition and Design in "The Iliad,"* Oxford, 1930. "T.E. Shaw" in his Translator's note to *The Odyssey*, Oxford, 1932, found "the fixed grin of archaism.") Indeed Philo Judaeus allegorized the relationship of Abraham and Isaac to produce the message, "God is the maker of laughter." *Quod Deterius Potiori Insidiari Soleat*, 33, 124, quoted by Harry A. Wolfson, *The Philosophy of the Church Fathers*, 3rd ed. (Cambridge, Mass.: Harvard University Press, 1970), 173. For a singularly grim account of the "cosmic laughter" or "divine humor" see Gregory Ziegelmaier, "The Comedy of *Paradise Lost*," *College English*, 26 (1965), 516–22. Henry More the Cambridge Platonist had his own "as if" version of Augustine: "As if Providence look'd upon her bringing Man into the World as a Spectatour of a Tragick–Comedy." *Divine Dialogues* (London, 1668), I, 180, quoted by C.A. Patrides, "The Comic Dimension in

Greek Tragedy and *Samson Agonistes*," *Milton Studies*, 10 (1977), 17 (an essay valuable for its points and references on the comic in Homer, Aeschylus, Sophocles, and Euripides). Anthony Low's last word on "*Elegia Septima*: The Poet and the Poem" is "*Chaucerian*"! *Milton Studies*, 19 (1984) 34.

19. Hephaestus, who trapped his wife and Ares, is now a devil.

> Aside the Devil turned
> For envy, yet with jealous leer malign
> Eyed them askance, and to himself thus plained:
>   "Sight hateful, sight tormenting! thus these two
> Imparadised in one another's arms"
>
>   (IV. 502–06).

Satan sounds like a cuckolded husband; he has indeed lost licit pleasure. In the myth it was the Sun that informed Hephaestus of the adultery. Ovid, in recounting the episode in *Ars Amatoria*, II. 573 ff. (he also told it in *Metamorphoses* IV. 169 ff.), asked, "Who could deceive the Sun?" The answer is that Satan "beguiled / Uriel, though regent of the Sun" (III. 689–90)--though not for long.

20. Namely, *Milton and Sex* (New York: Columbia University Press, 1978; London: The Macmillan Press).
21. He had it in 1937, 124.
22. Landor, II, 64. Pope's *Odyssey* (I. 22/IX. 32) twice took over IV. 311 for Calypso's constraining Ulysses. Noted by Barbara K. Lewalski, "On Looking into Pope's Milton," *Études Anglaises*, 27 (1974), 487.
23. Elledge, ed., *Paradise Lost* (New York: Norton, 1975), p. xiv.
24. Barbara Breasted, "*Comus* and the Castlehaven Scandal," *Milton Studies*, 3 (1971), 201–24. But see John Creaser, "Milton's *Comus*: The Irrelevance of the Castlehaven Scandal," *Milton Quarterly*, 21 (1987), 24–34.
25. W.B.C. Watkins, *An Anatomy of Milton's Verse* (Baton Rouge: Louisiana State University Press, 1955), 99. Not without ancient authority Simon Forman's Diary uses *virgam*--with or without *virilem*--for penis, as quoted by A.L. Rowse, *Simon Forman: Sex and Society in Shakespeare's Age* (London: Weidenfeld and Nicolson, 1974), 80–81.
26. J.W.Flosdorf, "'Gums of Glutinous Heat': A Query," *Milton Quarterly*, 7 (1973), 4–5; John T. Shawcross, "Two Comments," *Ibid.*, 98. These conjectures have not been excluded from *The Cambridge Companion to Milton*, ed., Dennis Danielson (Cambridge, 1989), 32. Milton showed a marginal interest in the semen of seals in two notes he made in a copy of Lycophron's *Alexandra* that he purchased in 1634, the year of *Comus*. See

Harris Francis Fletcher, "John Milton's Copy of Lycophron's *Alexandra* in the Library of the University of Illinois," *Milton Quarterly*, 23 (1989), 142–43. To get back to a more adhesive meaning of "seal," a sexual and sacramental pun has been seen in "of thir mutual guilt the Seale" (*PL* IX. 1044). Georgia B. Christopher, *Milton and the Science of the Saints* (Princeton: Princeton University Press, 1982), 162; George H. McLoone, "Milton's Twenty-Third Sonnet: Love, Death, and the Mystical Body of the Church," *Milton Quarterly*, 24 (1990), 17.

27.   This anonymous reaction was passed on to me: "This commentary on *Comus* is merely playing the game of the sexually-obsessed modern. Reference to orgasms and masturbation is totally irrelevant to the context." I have myself attacked finding sex in Milton where the context does not warrant it ("By Sex Obsessed," *Milton Quarterly*, 8 [1974], 55 ff. and cf. Note 40 below), but if *this* context is not sexual, what is it? What else can the lines mean? Or are we to wander vaguely as a cloud? Moreover, the autoerotic interpretation has been arrived at independently by three critics in recent years: first by Martin Fido in a fugitive magazine. *Oxford Review*, 1 (1966), 62. As I was writing, John Shawcross was putting into print the comment, "The reference to masturbation is obvious enough...." "Milton and Diodati: An Essay in Psychodynamic Meaning," *Milton Studies*, 7 (1975), 162, n. 31.

28.   Bush and A.S.P. Woodhouse, eds., *Variorum Commentary, The Minor English Poems* (New York: Columbia University Press, 1972), 948.

29.   *Ibid.*, 951. Compare with Milton's "cattle" references Robert Lowell's "We moved far, bull and cow, could one imagine / cattle obliviously pairing six long days." *Mexico*, 4, in *Selected Poems* (New York: Farrar, Straus, 1976), 196.

30.   *Complete Prose Works*, 2, volume editor Ernest Sirluck (New Haven: Yale, 1959), 445, 449, 460, 464, 465, 474. I have substituted quotation marks for Williams' parentheses.

31.   Harding, 48. Of course cases abound of innocence on both parts. To give an instance that seems not to have been recorded, there is "Lycidas," 102, "sacred head"--*caput...sanctum*, in the pseudo-Ovidian *Consolatio Ad Liviam*, 253. This is in the area of both poems where the Loeb Library editor found a resemblance--between mourning Tiber and mourning Cam. J.H. Mozley, ed., Ovid, *The Art of Love and Other Poems* (London: Heinemann, 1939), 339.

32.   Edward Phillips, "The Life of Mr. John Milton," in Darbishire, 66.

33.   The Latin text and translation are given by Leo Miller, *John Milton among the Polygamophiles* (New York: Loewenthal Press, 1974), 209–10.

34. Intervening are such expressions in Spenser as "bathe in pleasaunce" and "swimming in that sea of blissfull joy" (*Faerie Queene*, I, vii, 4. 2; xii. 41. 5).

35. Spitzer, "Marvell's `Nymph Complaining for the Death of Her Faun': Sources versus Meaning," first published in *Modern Language Quarterly*, 19 (1958), 231–43.

36. John M. Steadman, "Sin, Echidna and the Viper's Brood," *Modern Language Review*, 56 (1961), 65, n. 2.

37. *Pseudodoxia Epidemica*, Third Book, ch. 16, in *Works*, ed. G. Keynes, 2 (London: Faber and Gwyer, 1928), 238. Early in the nineteenth century that amateur naturalist De Witt Clinton recorded, in regard to rattlesnakes, the belief "that the young when wounded take refuge in the mother's belly." Vivian C. Hopkins, "The Empire State--De Witt Clinton's Laboratory," *New-York Historical Society Quarterly*, 69 (1975), 15.

38. Pindar, *Nemean Odes* IV, 68–70, trans. Sir John Sandys (London: Heinemann, Loeb Classical Library, 1937), 349.

39. For a conspectus see Ruth Mohl, *John Milton and His Commonplace Book* (New York: Ungar, 1969), 142–47. For historical background see Helmut Schoeck, *Envy: A Theory of Social Behavior* (New York: Harcourt, 1970).

40. But Shawcross does, "Milton and Diodati," 153–54. I literally cannot begin to follow Shawcross in his theory of the homosexuality of Milton and Diodati. He begins by translating line 216 of "Epitaphium Damonis," "*Laetaque frondentis gestans umbracula palmae*," as "and riding in happy bowers entwined with palm leaves" (127; also in his edition of *The Complete Poetry*, New York: Anchor, 1971, 193; earlier in *Complete English Poetry*, 1963, 143). Then he comments (128): "But Diodati does not simply rest in his bower: he is `riding' (`gestans'). The word has the obvious meaning of spinning round in his heavenly orbit like all angelic intelligences, but also the commonplace physical meaning of sexual intercourse." This might be interesting if *gestans* meant "riding," which it does not. All other Milton editors agree on the sense of the line, of which a literal translation is, "and bearing the joyful shades of the leafy palm." The reference is to Revelation 7.9, "palms in their hands" (in the Vulgate, "*palmae in manibus eorum*"). There is no linguistic indication that anybody is riding anything or anybody. I also cannot follow the conjectures of Latin double-entendre and the Freudian analysis of imagery (trees are male, water is female: a far cry from the scriptural allegorists, commencing with Barnabas, for whom water prefigured baptism, and trees the Cross). There is such a thing as not being able to see the wood, for the phalluses. New critics, putting on medieval lenses, have seen baptismal water in "Lycidas." Now the last line, "To-morrow to fresh woods, and

pastures new," has to face the inquiry, "Should the male symbol of *woods* and female symbol of *pastures* be especially noted?" (153). Speculative, introducing innovation myself, I realize it behooves me to have a high tolerance for the speculations of others, but there are limits. Even of the younger, more ambivalent Milton, my impression does not accord with A.L. Rowse's overall one that "he was not very heterosexual." *Milton the Puritan* (London: Macmillan, 1977), 69.

41.   E.P. Coleridge translation, *The Complete Greek Drama*, eds. W.J. Oates and Eugene O'Neill, Jr. (New York: Random House, 1938), I, 931. The latter part of this statement is, significantly, in harmony with the second of three quotations from Sallust on the title page of *Eikonoklastes* to the effect that kings are suspicious of good men, "and the merit of others is always a cause of fear *(formidolosa)* to them." *Bellum Catilinae*, VII.

42.   Le Comte, *Milton's Unchanging Mind* (Port Washington, N.Y.: Kennikat, 1973), 31–34.

43.   C.V. Wedgwood, *The King's War, 1641–1647* (London: Collins, 1958), 474. See also 130: "The distinction between Charles as a man and Charles as King seemed a dangerous sophistry. 'I beseech you to consider that Majesty is sacred,' wrote young Edmund Verney to his elder brother who had chosen to stay with Parliament, 'I believe ye will all say ye intend not to hurt the King, but can any of ye warrant any one shot to say it shall not endanger his very person?' A satirical parody of the Roundhead contention was crystallised in a piece of Cavalier ballad mockery: 'Tis to preserve His Majesty / That we against him fight.'"

44.   W.R. Parker, *Milton's Debt to Greek Tragedy in "Samson Agonistes"* (Baltimore: Johns Hopkins, 1937), 246. Cf. A.W. Verity, ed., *Samson Agonistes* (Cambridge: Pitt Press Series, 1892; 1966), xxxviii; Le Comte, *A Milton Dictionary* (1961; rpt. New York: AMS Press, 1969), 121, s.v. "Euripides"; Bush, *Mythology and the Renaissance Tradition*, 251. In the Renaissance Euripides was second only to Seneca. See, with references, Madeleine Doran, *Endeavors of Art: A Study of Form in Elizabethan Drama* (Madison: University of Wisconsin Press, 1954), 14–15.

45.   G.P. Gooch, *English Democratic Ideas in the Seventeenth Century* (1898; New York: Harper Torchbook, 1959), 150–51, quoting from *Behemoth* (1679), Dialogue I. For a pre-Bicentennial note: "the *American Magazine or a Monthly View of the Political State of the British Colonies* (Philadelphia) for January 1741, in its 'Plan of the Undertaking,' employs Milton's translation from Euripides prefixed to *Areopagitica*, p. viii." Shawcross, ed., *Milton 1732–1801: The Critical Heritage* (London: Routledge, 1972), 16.

46. William Haller, *Liberty and Reformation in the Puritan Revolution* (New York: Columbia University Press, 1955), 185. Even Christopher Hill concedes, "Milton was never a democrat." But the conjecture is made that Milton was "at least considering anti-monarchical sentiments which he did not find it expedient to express openly until 1649." *Milton and the English Revolution* (London: Faber and Faber, 1977), 91.

47. *The History of Britain. Works*, 10, 324. Quoted by Haller, 245.

48. *"Bacchare herba est ad depellendum fascinum." Commentarii*, ed., Georg Thilo (Hildesheim: Georg Olms, 1961), III, Fasc. I, 86. Cf. Fasc. II, 133, 477.

49. Up to and including *Variorum Commentary*, IV, *Paradise Regained*, ed. Walter MacKellar (New York: Columbia University Press, 1975); Burton Jasper Weber, *Wedges and Wings: The Patterning of "Paradise Regained"* (Carbondale: Southern Illinois University Press, 1975). The point was bound to elude Lewalski, *Milton's Brief Epic: The Genre, Meaning, and Art of "Paradise Regained"* (Providence: Brown University Press, 1966), 6, because, as her translation shows, she takes *parerent* as coming, not from *pareo*, "obey," but from *pario*, "provide"--which is metrically impossible.

50. The earliest piece of Christian literature outside the New Testament continues in the same vein. "Think, my dear friends, how the Lord offers us proof after proof that there is going to be a resurrection, of which He has made Jesus Christ the first-fruits by raising Him from the dead....take the fruits of the earth; how, and in what way, does a crop come into being? When the sower goes out and drops each seed into the ground, it falls to the earth shrivelled and bare, and decays; but presently the power of the Lord's providence raises it from decay, and from that single grain a host of others spring up and yield their fruit." Clement of Rome, "The First Epistle to the Corinthians," 24. *Early Christian Writings: The Apostolic Fathers*, trans. Maxwell Staniforth (Harmondsworth: Penguin, 1968), 36. Milton quoted from this newly discovered work (first published at Oxford in 1633), *The Reason of Church-Government, Works*, 3, 221; cf. 211.
    The next step was the compilation of dictionaries of biblical allegories, such as *Allegoriae in Universam Sacram Scripturam* by Rabanus Maurus (9th century), of which one entry reads: "*Ager* (field) is the world, as in the Gospel, `To the man who sowed good seed in his field,' that is to Christ, who sows preaching through the world." Quoted by Henry Osborn Taylor, *The Medieval Mind* (London: Macmillan, 1938), 2, 74. Compare the reference in *Areopagitica* to "the field of this World," *Works*, 4, 310. Four months earlier Roger Williams used a number of times "field of the

world" (the phrase derives from Mat. 13. 38) in *The Bloody Tenet of Persecution* in an elaborate and lengthy reinterpretation of the parable of the Tares (a parable also referred to in *Areopagitica*, 349). Excerpts in Woodhouse, ed., *Puritanism and Liberty: Being the Army Debates (1647–9) from the Clarke Manuscripts with Supplementary Documents* (Chicago: University of Chicago Press, 1951), 268–72.

51. For another possible Erasmian connection see Ch. VII of George W. Whiting, *Milton's Literary Milieu* (Chapel Hill: University of North Carolina Press, 1939), "*Comus* and *Encomium Moriae*," 242–50.

52. Consider, for instance, a parallel brought to my attention by a graduate student, Patricia Dougherty: "Home to his mother's house" (*Paradise Regained* IV. 639)--"Home to his father's house" (*Samson Agonistes* 1733). (I subsequently found it pointed to by Earl Miner, *The Restoration Mode from Milton to Dryden* [Princeton University Press, 1974], 287.) The Dagon–slayer and the Dragon–slayer have quiet exits, in accordance with Milton's pattern of quiet endings. Is the specific parallel insignificant, the poet just slipping into the same expression to begin two lines of blank verse? (How distinctive is the phrase? How distinctive is "Yet once more," "Lycidas," 1--Son. XXIII, 7--Hebrews 12: 26–27? Joseph A. Wittreich, Jr., ed., *Milton and the Line of Vision* [Madison: University of Wisconsin Press, 1975], 117–18, 122, is the latest to find that repetition highly meaningful.) Have we here one indication that *Paradise Regained* and *Samson Agonistes*, published together, are compositions close in time, as most scholars believe? (I have attacked W.R. Parker's heretical dating with "New Objections to a Pre–Restoration Date for *Samson Agonistes*," *Poets' Riddles: Essays in Seventeenth–Century Explication* [Port Washington, N.Y.: Kennikat, 1975], 129–60.) The typologist will say that Milton is dropping a hint (as with the Phoenix reference, 1699–1707) that Samson is a Christ–figure. "Home to his Father's House" (the original text capitalizes the *F* and has no apostrophe) means not only gathered to his father and his fathers, but gone to God the Father. Samson dead will be saved by the living Jesus, or the only transiently dead one in the Harrowing of Hell. "Then God by His might entered hell to the sons of men; He was minded to bring forth many thousands of men up to his home." ("Christ and Satan," *Anglo–Saxon Poetry*, selected and trans. R.K. Gordon [London: Dent, Everyman's Library, 1954], 131.) The critic may see a connection between two homes and two parents (Mary and Manoa) that could not provide full understanding of remarkable sons. The psychoanalyst's inference would be that, despite difficulties adumbrated in "Ad Patrem" (the Unconscious knows no time),

Milton felt, unlike his brother Christopher, that home was where he belonged and would stay--with mother and father. For once the father–centered (or Father–centered) Milton (a subordinationist in his view of the Trinity and of women) gives, first and last in *Paradise Regained,* a mother her due. Besides, he could not have wanted what would in Jesus' case have been not the profitable ambiguity but the sheer confusion of "Home to his father's house." And he is concerned, as MacKellar says (*Variorum Commentary,* 31), with "emphasizing Christ's humanity."

53.   Compare the hidden heresies (so hidden that there is no agreement as to what they are) in *Paradise Lost,* as commented on by B. Rajan, *"Paradise Lost" and the Seventeenth–Century Reader* (London: Chatto and Windus, 1947), 23 ff. "My claim will be that Milton seems to go out of his way to avoid harassing the reader with his personal beliefs and that in the effort to do so he 'tones down' his heresies as much as he can without being dishonest." Leonora Leet Brodwin, "The Dissolution of Satan in *Paradise Lost*: A Study of Milton's Heretical Eschatology," *Milton Studies,* 8 (1975), 165–207, makes a resolute attempt "to pierce the mist of ambiguity which almost obscures the heretical eschatology of *Paradise Lost*" (202). We are presented a sly Milton who sneaked in a heresy not even to be found in *De Doctrina Christiana.* "But if Milton avoids this particular heresy in his treatise, he introduces it into his epic through the same strategy of ambiguity and omission which marks his presentation of those heresies he does profess openly in the treatise, carefully constructing each eschatological statement to appear orthodox on the surface while admitting hidden heretical meaning" (166). "Though Milton couches this heresy in a strategy of careful ambiguity and omission, it permeates every aspect of the epic and is an index to its meaning. As hints of his radical eschatology are numerous and pointed, as Milton would not be likely to toy with theology on such a vital point, and as the heresy is developed with such astonishing consistentcy throughout *Paradise Lost,* it seems evident that Milton expressed his true eschatological belief, however covertly, in his epic rather than in his theological treatise" (190). Other telling expressions are: "the careful use of ambiguity and omission seems calculated as part of a consistent strategy of double meaning, the heresy hidden behind an appearance of orthodoxy" (192), and the query as to whether "he was being secretive about his agreement with Socinus on this point" (196). This is a Milton I have no trouble recognizing, whether or not Brodwin is right in her particular insistence.

For a very different instance, the hidden meaning of *forsaken* in 'Bring the rathe primrose that forsaken dies" ("Lycidas," 142), is likely to have something to do with "unwedded," which is what Milton first wrote in the Cambridge Manuscript. It is a struggle against odds to deny this as the following commentary does: "Milton in this passage makes some excisions that enhance the typological quality of the chosen flowers. C.S. Jerram pointedly observes that Milton discards the allusion in the delineation of the primrose to the fabled amours of the sun with various flowers—the sun in *Lycidas* is Christ in one aspect or another—and uses *forsaken* to suggest 'the modest nature of the flower, blooming in retired spots, and often fading unnoticed.' His first allusion to the primrose, long associated (cf. *Hamlet*, I, iii) with love, even sensual love, is much too florid for a funerary ceremony. It has been noted that some critics interpret *forsaken* as 'unwedded,' Milton's cancelled first choice; but the word may simply mean 'left alone': the primrose, according to W.A. Neilson, blooms in secluded places before other flowers. One may think that Milton means simply the lonely primrose...." David S. Berkeley, *Inwrought with Figures Dim: A Reading of Milton's 'Lycidas'* (The Hague: Mouton, 1974), 54. One may think that the primrose, like Edward King–Lycidas, if "lonely," is that for lack of a mate. Berkeley does not seem to have had time to consult *Variorum Commentary* 2, 711 (published two years before), in which Woodhouse noted that the discarded line "puts beyond doubt the Shakespearean derivation of Milton's primerose: 'pale primroses, / That die unmarried ere they can behold / Bright Phoebus in his strength (a malady / Most incident to maids)...' (*W. Tale* 4.4. 122–5)"; cf. J.B. Leishman, *Milton's Minor Poems* (University of Pittsburgh Press, 1969), 304. Berkeley's lengthy bibliography (which omits Leishman and the 1968 Carey and Fowler edition) should at least have included Henry H. Adams, "The Development of the Flower Passage in 'Lycidas,'" *Modern Language Notes*, 65 (1950), 468–72, who explained that in changing "unwedded" to "forsaken" and also in suppressing the next line in his manuscript, "colouring the pale cheeke of uninjoyd love," the poet wanted to conceal or reduce his debt to Shakespeare besides diminishing an erotic element inappropriate at this funereal juncture. But that King–Lycidas died (like a pale virgin) without the normal sexual fruition accounts for the introduction of "myrtles" (sacred to Venus: see *Variorum Commentary* 2, 639; Francis Peck, *New Memoirs of the Life and Poetical Works of Mr. John Milton* [London, 1740], 165) in line 2 and the compensatory reference (as would be given Diodati also) to Heavenly "nuptial" in line 176.

A conjecture worth a note is the possibility of a secondary meaning in "Him the Almighty Power / Hurled headlong flaming from th'ethereal sky / With hideous ruin and combustion down" (I. 44–46). There is no doubt of the primary meaning, signalled by the etymology of *ruin* and *combustion*--"fall" and "burning together." But does "With" introduce one of Milton's typically loose and ambiguous constructions: "With *his* hideous ruin and combustion" in reference to the truly hideous damage wrought by the enemy in Heaven? "And now all heav'n / Had gone to wrack, with ruin overspread, / Had not th' Almighty Father..." (VI. 669 ff.). Satan is burning as the recipient of God's lightning, but Lucifer had hurled missiles and burned gunpowder. Lucifer was a firebrand, and if one doesn't extinguish a firebrand one throws it out. I am led to this consideration by Milton's favorite Latin historian (cf. *Works* 12, 52, 100), Sallust. I have long felt there were parallels, including perversity of motive, between Satan and that arch Roman conspirator Catiline. (Compare the usual "mildness," VI. 735, of the Son with that of Julius Caesar proposing that the conspirator Lentulus should not be permitted to die, resulting in the verbal parallel--not source, for the Bible was Milton's source--of "driven down / To chains of darkness, and th'undying worm," VI. 738-9, with *Itaque homo mitissimus atque lenissimus non dubiat P. Lentulum aeternis tenebris vinculisque mandare*," Cicero, *In L. Catilinam Oratio IV*, 5 Actually, except as a grim pun, "worm"-- presumably "the ayenbite of inwyt"--does not fit the almost conscienceless devils, but it would fit Lentulus. As Jesus said of Tiberius, "Let his tormentor Conscience find him out," *Paradise Regained* IV. 130.) (Editors neglect Cicero, who used to be so familiar, to their loss. For Athens as "mother of arts / And eloquence, *Paradise Regained* IV. 240-1, MacKellar's *Variorum Commentary* 4, 200 does cite "Cicero (*Flac.* 26. 62)," but it is the wrong Cicero. Clearly Milton is translating De Oratore L4: "*Graeciam quae semper eloquentiae princeps esse voluit, atque illas omnium doctrinarum inventrices Athenas.*") At *Paradise Lost* I. 44-46, we have verbal connections with Catiline's reaction on being cornered in the Senate on the day Cicero delivered his First Oration against him. "*Tum ille furibundus `Quoniam quidem circumventus,' inquit, `ab inimicis praeceps agor, incendium meum ruina restinguam,*'" Sallust, *Bellum Catilinae* XXXI ("Then he exclaimed, in a fury, Since I am circumvented by my enemies and *am driven headlong*, I will extinguish my *fire* by a general *ruin*"). J.C. Rolfe, the Loeb Library editor (London: Heinemann, 1931, 55), explains, "He refers to the method of checking great fires by the demolition of buildings and the like." This was resorted to in the fire of London in 1666. If Milton had this striking quotation in mind, beginning with "*praeceps agor*," the secondary meaning outlined above tagged along with it. Anyone interested in comparing the characters of Catiline and Satan will get more from Cicero's *Pro Caelio*, V-VI, than from Ben Jonson's inert play

Catiline. (See rather, though it does not deal with Milton's Satan, Charles A. Hallett, "The Satanic Nature of Volpone," *Philological Quarterly*, 49 [1970], 41–55.) But Jonson does have, by way of Sallust, a remark not included in the *Variorum Commentary* on "Lycidas," 71, the parenthesis on the longing for Fame as "(That last infirmity of noble mind)." Sallust had remarked (in the same section, VII, from which Milton was to make a direct quotation: see note 41 above), "*tanta cupido gloriae incesserat.*" Sallust began XI with: "*Sed primo magis ambitio quam avaritia animos hominum exercebat, quod tamen vitium propius virtutem erat.*" This Jonson sufficiently summed in the Chorus at the end of Act III of *Catiline*: "ambition, that near vice / To virtue." But what English predecessor comes so close to "Lycidas," 71, as the labelling of "Ambition" by Cicero at III. ii. 14–15: "the last affection / A high mind can put off"? On the basis of so commonplace a thought (openly political with Dryden: "Desire of greatness is a godlike sin," *Absalom and Achitophel*, I. 372) I cannot claim Milton read *Catiline*; but if he did, line 644 of the Fifth Act, "His countenance was a civil war itself," could have been the stimulus for––and is an epigram of–– the warring emotions on Satan's face as he stands on Mount Niphates, IV. 114 ff. (Montaigne can be added to the collection of commonplaces. Following a sentence citing the ambition of Alcibiades and before one mentioning "fame," the French essayist says, in John Florio's 1603 translation, "This infirmity is happily excusable, in so strong and full a minde." "How One Ought to Governe His Will," *Essayes*, III. x [New York: Modern Library, n.d., 926]. Innocent users of Burton Stevenson's *Book of Quotations Classical and Modern* [London: Cassell, 1934], 623, no. 16––or even J.K. Hoyt, ed., *The Cyclopedia of Practical Quotations* [New York: Funk and Wagnalls, 1896], 385 b––should be apprised that the supposed perfect coincidence of "Lycidas," 71 with the manuscript play *Sir John van Olden Barnevelt* is based on an editorial mishap: see Samuel C. Chew, *Lycidas* and the Play of Barnavelt," *Modern Language Notes*, 38 [1923], 122. Stevenson's learning and industry are a continuous marvel, but he is capable of mixing up Lucan with Lucian: 632, no. 10.)

Source clarifies grammar. At "Lycidas," 70, "fame is the spur that the clear spirit doth raise," the *Variorum Commentary* does not raise the question of whether "clear spirit" is the object or the subject of "doth raise." But it gives a clue by gathering quotations illustrating a commonplace that, to quote Ovid (as I did in 1961 in editing *"Paradise Lost" and Other Poems*, New York: Mentor, New American Library, 406), "Fame has a spur" (*Ex Ponto* IV. ii. 36). I can add a plural from Petrarch, "Trionfo del Tempo": "Or perchè umana gloria hà tante corna." P.L. Ginguené, ed., *Les*

Oeuvres Amoureuses (Paris: Garnier, n.d.) 376. I don't suppose these horns have any more to do with cuckoldry than the horns of Michelangelo's Moses, yet the burden (also a commonplace) of both poems happens to be that one is cheated by or of earthly fame.

Looking again at an old college text, Lucan, *De Bello Civile, VII*, ed., J.P. Postgate (Cambridge University Press, 1913), I can proffer a third explanation for a crux that Hughes in 1957 decided to ignore. (Students should be alerted that he dropped many a good note when he combined his three earlier volumes into one.) The Tempter is telling Jesus how far behind he is in accomplishment: "...young Pompey quelled / The Pontic king and in triumph had rode." *Paradise Regained*, III. 35–36. The fact is that Pompey "conquered Mithridates at forty, and rode in triumph in Rome at forty–five. So either the Devil is proving himself the father of lies or Milton in his sixties thinks forty–five 'young.' Need we choose, both being so plausible?" So I wrote in "Milton versus Time," *Milton's Unchanging Mind*, 47. But a third possibility is that Milton took poetic license from Lucan, who also mixed up Pompey's three triumphs, which were for Africa in 81 B.C., for Spain in 71, and for Asia (Mithridates) in 61. Lucan takes the second as the first (just as Milton treats the third as the youthful first) when he has Pompey on the eve on Pharsalia look back to "that distant past when, as a youth, at the time of his first triumph": *"olim cum iuuenis primique aetate triumphi, / post domitas gentes quas torrens ambit Hiberus, / et quaecumque fugax Sertorius impulit arma,"* etc. (VII. 14 ff.). Postgate comments dryly (xii), "[W]e might reasonably expect him to know the occasion of his hero's first triumph." Lucan did know that Pompey had three: VII. 685; VIII. 553, 814; IX. 599–600. Milton may be slyly conveying (or have privately concluded) that one poet's poetic license is good for another. One is allowed certain liberties for certain effects, as in saying (quite inaccurately) that "Charlemain with all his peerage fell / By Fontarabbia" (*Paradise Lost*, I. 586–87).

At *Paradise Lost* VII, 32 ff., where Milton identifies himself with Orpheus, what is the missing element and what is the missing source of, "nor could the Muse defend / Her son"? Milton's borrowing from himself goes back to "Lycidas," 58 ff., "What could the Muse herself that Orpheus bore," and, nine years before that, to El. VII. 45, *"Nec te, stulte, tuae poterunt defendere Musae."* But the commentators haven't had a great deal of luck in finding a source for the idea (which, to be sure, the poet was capable of arriving at independently). ("*Quid mater profuit Orpheo?*" *Amores* III. ix. 21, doesn't perhaps ring enough bells: *pace* John M. Major, "Ovid's *Amores* III. ix: A Source for Lycidas," *Milton Quarterly*, 6 [1972], 1–3.) Carey cites the epigram, VII. 8, of the *Greek*

Anthology, attributed to Antipater of Sidon. W.R. Paton's translation in the Loeb Library (London: Heinemann, 1917), vol. 2, 7–9, reads: "No more, Orpheus, shalt thou lead the charmed oaks and rocks and the shepherdless herds of wild beasts. No more shalt thou lull to sleep the howling winds and the hail, and the drifting snow, and the roaring sea. For dead thou art; and the daughters of Mnemosyne bewailed thee much, and before all thy mother Calliope. Why sigh we for our dead sons, when not even the gods have power to protect their children from death?" With the last eight Greek words Paton has not been literal enough for my purpose. Read: "since to ward off from their children Hades, not even to the gods is there power." *Hades* (capitalized in the original) is a provocative missing element (Antipater doesn't subscribe to the story that Orpheus' spirit reached the Elysian Fields), inasmuch as Milton has shown his horror of his own created Hell, felicitating himself on having "Escaped the Stygian pool" (III. 14) and being safely in the presence of Light: "Thee I revisit safe" (21). At VII, "More safe I sing" (24), *he hopes*, but cannot help remembering that Orpheus suffered the simultaneous, synonymous fate (for the ancients) of death (by assault) *and* Hades. Such would be an addendum to Alastair Fowler's observation, "The myth of [Orpheus'] dismemberment by Thracian women during orgies of Bacchus seems to have focused some of M[ilton]'s deepest fears." Ed., with John Carey, *The Poems of John Milton* (London: Longmans, 1968), 777. Orpheus, like Milton, came back with personal safety from Hell once; there was a young carefree time when this was the only phase of Orpheus' career that the English poet mentioned: "L'Allegro," 145 ff.; "Il Penseroso," 105 ff. Milton, at twenty-five, wrote "Stygian poole" as part of the opening lines of his *Mask*, but, escapist, he crossed it out. *Works*, I, 479; W.A. Wright, ed., *Facsimile of the Manuscript of Milton's Minor Poems* (Cambridge University Press, 1899), 10. The expression had been used a hundred years before *Paradise Lost* in John Studley's translation, 1566, of Seneca's *Agamemnon*. In Eric C. Baade, ed., *Seneca's Tragedies* (New York: Macmillan, 1969), 129. Milton scholars have emerged from the library with perhaps too much of the allegorical and typological Orpheus, leading us away from an exceedingly personal symbol. (I agree with Bush: "Milton did not apparently accept the typological Orpheus," *Pagan Myth and Christian Tradition in English Poetry* [Philadelphia: American Philosophical Society, 1968], 24.) Consider the assertion in *Reason of Church-Government* that hymns (like those attributed to Orpheus?) can "allay the perturbations of the mind" (*Works*, 3, 238). Milton worked through hymning at allaying his. If we're going in for allegory I prefer the psychologically suggestive one of George

Chapman, who used the same phrase of Orpheus. (*Perturbatio* was the Renaissance rendition of Aristotle's *pathos*: see Steadman, *Epic and Tragic Structure in "Paradise Lost,"* University of Chicago Press, 1976, 79 ff.) Orpheus—poetry—quells fears, fears of darkness and the deep: "And that in calming the infernal kind, / To wit, the perturbations of his mind, / And bringing his Eurydice from hell / (Which justice signifies) is proved well." *The Shadow of Night* (1594), "Hymnus in Noctem," in *Works: Poems and Minor Translations* (London: Chatto and Windus, 1875), 6. A more historical personage could also have figured in Milton's perturbations: Hesiod, murdered and cast into the sea, where his body, escorted by dolphins, came to shore near Oenoë in Locris. Independently, J. Martin Evans has made the same conjecture: "Lycidas and the Dolphins," *Notes and Queries*, NS 25 (1978), 15–17.

Finally, as I pointed out in a review of Leo Miller's *John Milton and the Oldenburg Safeguard* (*JEGP*, 86 [1986], 251–54), there is the case of the difficult handwriting of a correspondent, Hermann Mylius, which Milton and his editors could have deciphered by identifying a quotation's source. Mylius to Milton, LIII, was first printed in the Columbia *Works*, 12. 356, with a photographic facsimile of the First Draft facing. A poet not identified has Hecuba lamenting: "Regina olim, nunc *secius*." In this reading "secius" is an adverb, "once queen, now changed" (358–59). J. Milton French, *Life Records of John Milton*, 3 (New Brunswick, N.J.: Rutgers University Press, 1954), 144–47 reads "seruia" (one would expect *serva*): "now a slave." The Yale translators follow this (4. 840). Miller, 137–39 has it as "servio": "now I slave.' So it is an adverb versus a noun versus a verb. Location of the source of the quotation is needed. It appears that these and the following words, "Exul deserta, afflictissima hominum," are a translation of Hecuba's speech to Agamemnon in Euripides, *Hecuba*, lines 809 and 811. E.P. Coleridge's version reads: "I was once a queen, but now I am thy slave;...reft of city, utterly forlorn, the most wretched woman living." Mylius' Latin translation was not original with him. If Milton, with what eyesight still remained, had trouble with this part of his correspondent's wretched handwriting, all he had to do was to consult—or have consulted—his copy of the Paulus Stephanus bilingual edition of Euripides (Geneva, 1602), which survives in the Bodleian with his notes (see *JEGP*, 60 [1961], 680–87). The translation by Canterus of line 811 is identical with Mylius'. Its line 809 is: "Regina etam olim, but nunc serva tua." Heidelberg, 1597 had the same (but Stiblinus, 1562, and Erasmus, 1567, were different).

AMBIGUOUS MILTON

When Shakespeare in Sonnet CVII says, "The mortal moon hath her eclipse endured," we do not know what he means. There are many theories, as with the sonnets generally. He could be referring to the defeat in 1588 of the Spanish Armada, which sailed in a crescent formation. He could be alluding to Queen Elizabeth, the chaste Diana. In that case there are two meanings of "endured" to consider. If it means "lived through," she survived her dangerous "climacteric" year when she became sixty-three in 1596; or she survived a dangerous illness in 1599, or the Essex rebellion of 1601. If "eclipse" means death, that took place March 24, 1603. Or should we look for an eclipse of the real moon, called "mortal" for suffering it: the total eclipse of 1595? Shakespeare knew what he meant--it goes without saying--but he was not writing for the public; he did not intend his sonnets to be published. They were circulated in manuscript "among his private friends." Topical allusions for the most part had to be discreet, references to the Queen guarded: otherwise one could go to jail. Writing sonnets was a cryptic game, anyway, as the connoisseurs knew.

When Milton in Sonnet VII says, "How soon hath Time, the subtle thief of youth, / Stolen on his wing my three-and-twentieth year," we do not know what birthday he is commemorating. Is it his twenty-third, or his twenty-fourth? The heading found in many editions, "On Being Arrived at Twenty-three Years of Age," has no authority, dates from the eighteenth century. If Milton's twenty-third year is gone, then he is twenty-four. Judging by the author's Latin practice, he means by "my three-and-twentieth year" "the year in which I was twenty-three," and thus wrote his "Petrarchian stanza" (as he called it) on or soon after his twenty-fourth birthday, December 9, 1632. Shall we say that Milton was simply not a mathematician? He said of the Marchioness of Winchester, "Summers three times eight save one / She had told"--which is not accurate: she had lived through twenty-four summers, although she was still twenty-three when she died. The *History of Britain* states that

83

Tugarus expired "in the 115th year" of his age, but the Latin source says that that monk had completed a span of 115 years.

Not all scholars go along with the modern reversal of opinion that makes the birthday of the sonnet Milton's twenty-fourth. Maybe the earlier view which took the only figure given without getting complicated about it was right. It is unfortunate that the author himself did not bestow upon it an unmistakable heading. He would have done so if he had realized there was a problem. He has not Shakespeare's reasons, or any conceivable reason, to be cryptic. In a poem he published twice he is pointing to an important milestone, sharing with his readers his anxiety about what he called in a letter "a certain belatedness in mee" that, the sestet concludes, the great Task-Master will not be too harsh on. We try to make out the milestone, but which of two figures is on it? Milton neglected to write clearly. It is not the reader who is obtuse; if anything, he is too acute.

For all its autobiographical interest and unquestioned sincerity, the sonnet is riddled from beginning to end with obscurities that, if it were a freshman composition, we would not hesitate to red-pencil. Consider the last six lines:

> Yet be it less or more, or soon or slow,
> It shall be still in strictest measure even
> To that same lot, however mean or high,
> Toward which Time leads me, and the will of Heaven;
> All is, if I have grace to use it so,
> As ever in my great Task-Master's eye.

We have "it" thrice: the antecedent of the first is doubtful, and so is the antecedent of the third. Is "even" an adjective or an adverb? It depends upon punctuation (lacking in Milton's manuscript), and the meaning would be different. On the last two lines the *Variorum Commentary* remarks, "Editors have been generally silent on these lines, which are not easy to interpret with certainty." Blithe and debonair, the Summer 1982 issue of *ELH* puts some readers' minds to rest (but not mine): "it does not matter what the last two lines mean."

Going back to "it," more often than not the reference is taken to be to "inward ripeness" (line 7), but that is to build on sand, for what does that line mean? "And inward ripeness doth much less appear." Is Milton saying that he has inward ripeness, but it cannot be seen? Or, on the contrary, is he confessing to a lack of inward ripeness, which is why it cannot be seen? In the latter case "appear" means "start to bloom," and is consistent with line 4: "But my late spring no bud or blossom shew'th."

Milton is supposed to be the very epitome of careful art. He is the opposite of the natural genius Shakespeare, untutored, fast-writing, never blotting a line, careless in little things. The one poet envied the other his ease of composition: "For whilst to the shame of slow–endeavoring art / Thy easy numbers flow"; "sweetest Shakespeare, Fancy's child, / Warble his native wood–notes wild." It surely would never be said of Milton, the classically clear contriver, what Johnson said of Shakespeare: "It is incident to him to be now and then entangled with an unwieldy sentiment, which he cannot well express, and will not reject; he struggles with it a while, and if it continues stubborn, comprises it in words such as occur, and leaves it to be disentangled and evolved by those who have more leisure to bestow upon it."

But if Milton is so classically clear, why has he left his readers so many puzzles? Why has he left us the biggest crux in English literature, one that surpasses "runaways' eyes" in *Romeo and Juliet* or "eisel" in *Hamlet* (for neither of which the author may be responsible)? I refer not to *haemony*, the mysteriously named magic plant of *Comus* (modelled on Homer's moly), on which so much ink has been spilt, for that is apparently cryptic on purpose, an experiment in Spenserian allegory. The biggest crux of course is lines 130–31 of "Lycidas." The odds are that Milton had something definite in mind when he had St. Peter say, "But that two–handed engine at the door / Stands ready to smite once, and smite no more." We are expected to recognize an allusion, as is indicated by "that," Latin *ille*, "the famous." It is a powerful and concrete image. Is it a long sword, like that wielded by Michael in *Paradise Lost* "with huge two–handed sway"? Is it a battering–ram? Is it an axe? A clock? St. Peter's "two massy keys" (line 110)? A lock? A man? Two hands in prayer? A sheephook? A scales? The "abhorrèd shears" of the blind Fury (line 75)? The two houses of Parliament? The Old and New Testament? The two nations of England and Scotland? The scythe of Time? The flail of Talus? The rod of Christ? A spear? The club of Hercules? To date there have been fifty conjectures, the latest emanating from the Sorbonne in 1982: the bow–and–arrow of God, with a benign aspect as God's rainbow! (See Appendix.) If we have no preference, some recommend a conflation. Perhaps the most amusing suggestion is that it is the *crux* itself, which means cross, but I doubt if Milton has chosen this occasion to thumb his nose at future commentators. Some interpretations seem sillier than others, but again this is only opinion, as we jeer at each other, all equally in the dark.

Is "Lycidas" the better for being inexplicable at a crucial juncture? The lovers of the apocalyptic will say yes. The rest of us, despite the ample opportunity we have been vouchsafed to speculate and publish, will not make a virtue of what was not necessary and will acknowledge that a failure to communicate has taken place, a failure that is the writer's egocentric fault.

Probably in 1658, the same writer, now blind and with greater temptations than ever to self–absorption, composed a sonnet to his deceased wife. It is almost unbearably tender, a side too seldom revealed.

Carried away by his dream and his dream-production, Milton neglected to anticipate a mundane question posterity would have. Maybe it is a silly question, but some have raised it and the author could easily have scotched it. He had two deceased wives behind him. Which one was he writing about--Mary, or Katherine? One critic has proposed conflation here, too, and said both, and another has said neither but rather an ideal, but to me such evasions are desperate nonsense. Blame Milton for not being unmistakable: again, a heading would have done it.

The beguiling "L'Allegro" trips into grammatical confusion:

> And if I give thee honor due,
> Mirth, admit me of thy crew,
> To live with her, and live with thee,
> In unreprovèd pleasures free;
> To hear the lark begin his flight,
> And singing startle the dull night,
> From his watch-tower in the skies,
> Till the dappled dawn doth rise;
> Then to come in spite of sorrow
> And at my window bid good-morrow.

Who comes or is to come? Is it the lark? Is it L'Allegro himself? Is it Mirth? Or dawn? Or night? This became the subject of a lively and prolonged correspondence in the London *Times Literary Supplement* in 1934, involving, among others, some of the leading critics of the day. Things grew rancorous as each defended his position. The last letter, before the editors declared they could print no more, came from a schoolteacher in Cardiganshire who reported that his classes "invariably and without noticing any difficulty understand the lines." It is apparently quite easy not to notice any difficulty, and also to be swept along without fussing over details, or caring about contradictions or ambiguities when they are pointed out. One can always resort to conflation or to saying with a recent commentator that "Milton does not wish to bind us to any one of these interpretations." How happy to dance unbound, footloose and fancy-free, no raps from the schoolmaster about grammar! But Milton *was* a schoolmaster, a severe schoolmaster, who (just like ordinary mortals) did not always practise what he preached, and here is writing loosely, *not* on purpose.

Nor is the poem any better for a doubtful line a little further on: "And every shepherd tells his tale." Are the shepherds exchanging stories of love? Or are they counting their sheep (*tally* or even "tail") as shepherds were required to do at least once a day? There is no context to guide us. The poet meant one or the other, not both.

I am afraid this is an oft-repeated tally or tale. We cannot get past the opening of the "Song: On May Morning" without stumbling. "Now the bright morning star, day's harbinger, / Comes dancing from the east, and leads with her...." Of the two editors of the *Variorum Commentary* the first says, "The *morning star* is here, plainly, the sun." The second editor adds in brackets, "This seems hardly possible." His objection is that this star is feminine and therefore must be Venus or Lucifer (not that Lucifer sounds feminine). But a third interpretation will do as well: Aurora, the dawn. To add to the confusion, "Lucifer" in the Nativity Hymn may be the morning star or may be (as it is in two of the Latin elegies) the sun. So much for a poet praised for the exactitude of his astronomical references.

His mythological allusions can leave us alternatives that he did not have in mind when he wrote and that he would not have wanted us scurrying after. Take the reference in "Il Penseroso" to "that starred Ethiop queen that strove / To set her beauty's praise above / The sea-nymphs, and their powers offended." Here is "that" meaning famous again––Cassiopeia, turned into a constellation. The more familiar version of the myth has Cassiopeia boasting of her daughter's beauty, Andromeda's, not her own. She may still be doing this, if (as I am the first to suggest) Milton means by "beauty" what he means by it in "L'Allegro" (as well as in *Paradise Regained*): "Where perhaps some beauty lies"––i.e., a beautiful woman. But we do not know.

We do not know what "the sacred well" is in the invocation in "Lycidas": "Begin then, Sisters of the sacred well / That from beneath the seat of Jove doth spring." It could be the Pierian spring, with "the seat of Jove" being Mount Olympus. It could be Hippocrene, in which case "the seat of Jove" is Helicon, "the Aonian mount" of *Paradise Lost*. Or it could be Aganippe, another spring of Helicon. Declining these pagan choices, another critic turns to Revelation for "a pure river of water of life...proceeding out of the throne of God."

This is not the only hill of difficulty in "Lycidas." "Where were ye Nymphs?" "For neither were ye playing on the steep / Where your old bards, the famous Druids, lie." There are at least half a dozen conjectures as to what that steep is.

Passing from Latin or Greek to a less inflected language, Milton fails to realize that it is not necessarily self-evident whether a noun is the subject or the object of a verb. A famous line in "Lycidas" gets passed over without analysis: "Fame is the spur that the clear spirit doth raise / (That last infirmity of noble mind) / To scorn delights, and live laborious days." Does the spur "raise"––that is, lift up or impel––the clear spirit, or does the clear spirit grow or develop a spur? Ovid's "gloria calcar habet" is not decisive.

Ponder the line in "On Time": "And glut thyself with what thy womb devours." Is "womb" the object of "devours"? Time devours the (previously mentioned) Hours, which themselves devour the offspring of

Time, i.e., temporal things. Or does "womb" mean stomach? (*OED* meaning 1, now obsolete.) Gluttonous Time devours all.

Returning to the sonnets of Milton's middle period, we confront a number of useless riddles. "Lawrence, of virtuous father virtuous son" does not identify which of two sons is addressed, Edward or Henry. Worse, we are left to struggle with contradictory interpretations of the last two lines: "He who of those delights can judge, and spare / To interpose them oft, is not unwise." What does "spare to interpose them oft" mean? Does it mean spare *time* to interpose those delights often, or does it on the contrary convey a warning against interposing them often? For "spare" can mean "forbear," "refrain from." The latter usage is not only good Latin (*parcere* plus the infinitive), which would be reason enough for this author, but good literary English. Here, then, is a contest between meaning 8c of "spare" in the *Oxford English Dictionary*, "afford," and meaning 6c, "forbear." Is Milton being a right jolly good fellow, or is he issuing a warning against overindulgence? Too bad he failed to let us know.

What sort of comparison is being made in: "Thy age, like ours, O soul of Sir John Cheke, / Hated not learning worse than toad or asp, / When thou taught'st Cambridge and King Edward Greek." Take your pick of opposite paraphrases: (1) Your age did not hate learning as ours does. (2) Many men in that age (which has been thought so propitious to such studies) "hated not learning worse than toad or asp"--but as much as they hated either.

What is attached to what in the following sonnet "To the Lady Margaret Ley"? "Though later born than to have known the days / Wherein your father flourished, yet by you, / Madam, methinks I see him living yet/" "Though later born"--does it go with "I"? Or does it go with "you"? The date of this lady's birth is unknown.

Meanwhile Milton had been writing prose with what he called his left hand, with mixed results. This was one time he ignored etymology, prose from *prorsus*, meaning straightforward discourse. He had had no practice and no accepted model. He commences his first pamphlet, *Of Reformation in England*, with a self-revealing phrase, "Amidst those deep and retired thoughts." The trouble with deep and retired thoughts is, how do you transmit them? The first sentence consists of 146 words, and the second goes on for 375. Someone published an article designed to help the reader fight his way out of those two sentences, but the editor of the *Yale Prose*, without citing or using that, is content to rhapsodize, "Notice the richness of this sentence" (the first). Anyone who has tried to outline the famous *Areopagitica* (yes, even that) will remain on this side of idolatry as regards its structure.

Certainly Milton started out as a Ciceronian rather than a Senecan. What a contrast his convolutions are to the way his opponent, Bishop Hall, opened *Episcopacy by Divine Right*, viz.: "Good God! What is this I have lived to hear?" Milton was outraged at "a coy flirting style" that we might praise as modern. He found it intolerable "to be girded with frumps and curtal gibes by one who makes sentences by the statute, as if all above three inches long were confiscate."

So Milton's left hand produces a foot. I am not, however, making a choice between styles. I am not asking Milton to be modern, like us. Much of my pleasure in reading him comes from relishing what is not modern. But I do ask for clarity and refuse to praise unintended obscurity as a virtue.

For all their professional bias in favor of their author, the editors of the *Yale Prose* admit puzzlement in pamphlet after pamphlet. *Of Reformation* has a reference to "Clemens" that could be Clement of Rome, though it more likely is Clement of Alexandria. The next pamphlet, *Of Prelatical Episcopacy*, occasions a note: "Whether Milton is referring to...or to...is not clear." The third tract, *Animadversions upon the Remonstrant's Defence against Smectymnuus*, wrings from the learned editor the admission: "We are unable to identify the book here cited by Milton." *The Reason of Church–Government Urged against Prelaty* gets this note: "No example of an emblem in this form has been observed; it is likely that Milton had no specific emblem in mind." Another note starts: "This confused sentence seems to mean...." In the fifth and last of the anti–prelatical tracts, *An Apology* (to cut short a seventeen–word title), Yale has a *tu quoque* for the author: "A sentence no less complex than the one Milton has just objected to." Worse is the absence of any attention to a notable ambiguity. (One recalls Edward Young: "How commentators each dark passage shun, / And hold their farthing candle to the sun!") I mean the conclusion of the eloquent sentence: "Thus from the laureate fraternity of poets riper years and the ceaseless round of study and reading led me to the shady spaces of philosophy, but chiefly to the divine volumes of Plato and his equal Xenophon." Is Milton saying that Xenophon is equal in genius to Plato? The specialist, who knows there are two books on Milton and Plato and none on Milton and Xenophon, will deny this, as will any modern comparer. "Equal" can mean "the contemporary of," "one approximately the same age as," and is used in this sense a few paragraphs earlier. Milton never considered that he was sowing confusion. After all, he is mentioning the two authors in the same breath, he recommends their "moral works" together in *Of Education*, and Renaissance taste is not the same as ours. Spenser put Xenophon above Plato in one respect, and a recent commentator has argued that Milton regarded them as equally great in their different branches of wisdom.

Of Education recommends the study of logic and rhetoric: "To which Poetry would be made subsequent, or indeed rather precedent." So which is it? A 1989 commentator is right to be exasperated: "anyone wishing to implement Milton's programme might well stumble over the words...Do the boys read poetry after studying logic and rhetoric, or before?"

A computer-based statistical analysis of Milton's prose style has confirmed the impression that the luxuriance of his anti-prelatical pamphlets is replaced in later works "by a more sober style, a plainer medium for exposition." Let us leap, then, from the 1640's to the summer of 1659 and the Preface to *Considerations Touching the Likeliest Means to Remove Hirelings out of the Church*, where he addressed the Rump Parliament as

> next, under God, the authors and best patrons of religious and civil liberty that ever these lands brought forth. The care and tuition of whose peace and safety, after a short but scandalous night of interruption, is now again by a new dawning of God's miraculous providence among us revolved upon your shoulders.

One historian calls it "a staggering phrase," the indignant words, "a short but scandalous night of interruption." But for clarity it might just as well be the two-handed engine. Is it that Milton is giving the back of his hand, now, in abrupt reversal, to the Cromwellian Protectorate he had served so long? The Rump's lapse of power was six years: can that be called "short"? A second interpretation that has the merit of fitting "short" is the two weeks between the army's closing down of Richard Cromwell's parliament and the reinstallation of the Rump. A third interpretation frees Oliver Cromwell from Milton's sudden opprobrium and confines it to Richard's eight-month tenure. The statement, one of the most powerful of the author's side-swipes, is an irreplaceable key to his political attitude at this momentous juncture of history--but we do not know what lock it fits. He might as well be John on Patmos.

The ambiguities and puzzles we have been reviewing in the minor poems and the prose are indefensible. Blind idolatry must not say that they do not exist or praise these faults as virtues. The mystification is unintended, pointless, of no esthetic value even accidentally, and the solutions are mutually exclusive. The author, self-centered, did not realize he could be misunderstood. But with the great last poems the picture changes. With the good old cause lost, one would think that the Milton of the Restoration, blind and with all political and ecclesiastical hopes lost, "In darkness, and with dangers compassed round," would feel more isolated than ever and would have commensurately greater difficulty communicating his deep and retired thoughts.

I have catalogued in a book the ambiguities of *Paradise Lost, Paradise Regained*, and *Samson Agonistes*, which by my count number respectively 1203, 73, and 94. Most of these, whether intended or a critic's speculation, are puns of vocabulary or syntax that are advantageous on the hypothesis that two meanings that do not exclude each other are better than one.

Only a few problems of the bad old kind remain. Milton seems determined to leave us choosing between wives. In line 320 of *Samson Agonistes*, "To seek in marriage that fallacious bride," is the reference to Samson's first bride, the woman of Timnath, or to Dalila (who is Samson's wife in the play, though not in the Bible)? When Jesus in *Paradise Regained* retorts to Satan, "Tempt not the Lord thy God," does "thy God" mean "me" (he is revealing his identity) or "my God" (Jesus' Heavenly Father)? Theologically the difference may not be important, but dramatically it is. On the precise identity of the muse invoked in *Paradise Lost*, Urania, there have been ten conjectures. But probably it does not matter, as one meaning shades into another. "The meaning, not the Name, I call." Many meanings are called up, but no one need be chosen. As Aristotle observed, one can ask for only as much precision as the subject matter allows, and *Paradise Lost* has an airiness, a tendency to the vague sublime, that we can no more bind than, not being Aeolus, we can bind the winds.

Paradise Lost makes a virtue of ambiguity: "Of Man's first disobedience, and the fruit / Of that forbidden tree, whose mortal taste / Brought death into the world...." "Man" contains both the specific and the generic: mankind and Adam (Hebrew for man). "First," besides meaning earliest, may mean "most important." "Fruit" is the apple but also "outcome, consequences, fruition," as confirmed by a line in Book X, "Bad fruit of knowledge." Hidden in the word is *enjoyment* (Latin *fruor*), and there may be an allusion to the ceremony of firstfruits of Leviticus. "Mortal" means "deadly," but also "human"--taste by humans. Whether "taste" has *test* in it is more speculative.

One could go on, as I did in my *Dictionary*, to twelve hundred other instances. The poet has what in Freshman Composition would be condemned as dangling participles: in Latin they would be attached, showing number, case, perhaps gender. In the grand, free-floating style of this epic it does not bother the close reader that I think we should all be (but too few are) that he cannot parse the following: "Heaven opened wide / Her ever-during gates, harmonious sound / On golden hinges moving." Everything hinges, so to speak, on "moving." Is it an intransitive, a nominative absolute with "sound," meaning *in motion*? Is it a transitive, with "sound" as the object, meaning *causing*? (What does the moving: "heaven," or "gates"?) Finally, "moving" could be an intransitive that modifies "hinges": on moving golden hinges. We are happy not to know.

I have room here for just one more example of the enigmatic beauty of this style, the description of Belial: "A fairer person lost not heaven," which could also be read as, "Heaven lost not a fairer person." In Latin there would be no doubt as to whether "person" is the object or subject of "lost," but Milton's amphibology takes advantage of English's lack of inflection. And the editors have failed to notice one of the finest of his puns in "person," which remembers the derivation from *persona*, mask, Belial being a consummate hypocrite.

So Milton passed from ambiguity as, too, often, auctorial inattentiveness to his audience, to ambiguity as high art. Not at all incidentally, *Paradise Lost* is, as the latest biographer has remarked, "the least egotistical of his works."

The mining of meaning goes on. In 1990 *Milton Quarterly* (24, 111) Gregory Machacek caught a cunning pun that had eluded the commentators. Since "the Hebrew word for woman means *of man*," "of-man's first disobedience" means Eve's (cf. VIII, 494–7).

APPENDIX

Something Old and Something New
on That Two-Handed Engine

Oliver Lutaud's obliquely presented "Arc de Guerre ou d'Alliance" is the latest new conjecture. But publication continues and apparently will till the day of doom. It seems compulsory for the specialist (and also some outside amateurs) to enter the controversy. None more guilty than I, who (besides some references in other publications) had a main go at it in 1950, 1952, and 1975. Dr. Johnson puts us all on notice: "Conjecture has all the joy and all the pride of invention, and he that has once started a happy change, is too much delighted to consider what objections may rise against it."

The latest publication, in the Spring 1983 *Explicator*, has nothing new and much that is easily objected to. It shakes any faith in the idea of progress in scholarship and rapidly dissolves the delusion that the latest must be the best and truest. It is a rehash, or even a hash. It comes out in favor of St. Peter's keys. This was a suggestion I made in 1950 but immediately discarded, because the repeated "smite" seems to call for an instrument that smites literally as well as figuratively, and because if St. Peter were referring to something he was himself carrying, he would say, not "that two-handed engine." but "this two-handed engine." He is still the speaker, and the normal use of denotation, of "this" and "that," is not suspended because it is a poem. (The same objections apply to the *very* latest, which has just come to hand and takes another step backwards, in the May 1984 *Milton Quarterly*.)

The 1983 author does not deal with either of these previously published objections. Moreover, he muddies the waters by also claiming a reference too quiet and improbably papistical, namely the pope's heraldic device. "Should the reader question whether Milton would have portrayed the papal arms when he was so critical at times of the Roman church, the answer is that, aesthetically, the emblem's baroque implications outweighed the Romanist effect, one politically anathema to the poet." This is the Idol of the Cave. As Bacon said, "Men become attached to certain particular sciences and speculations, either because they fancy themselves the authors and inventors thereof, or because they have bestowed the greatest pains upon them and become most habituated to them." The author published in 1973 "The 'Two-Handed Engine': a Heraldic Emblem," and, though doubts seep in, how can he take it back ten years later? [The same author is still going strong--I should say, weak--in 1989/90 *Greyfriar*, "suggesting that the time lapse in between the mention of the keys and the engine allows for the demonstrative *that*. But another explanation is also possible: Peter is not referring to the keys as he is bearing them, but to their *crossed* position near the entrance of a

door, thus in heraldic terms: Milton thus shifts his focus temporarily [!]
from the individual to the more abstract."]

If popularity counts, for two centuries the sword has been (as the
Variorum Commentary notes) "the favourite image" for the crux.
Logically it would be a two-handed sword, a once widely used weapon.
Milton, who has a habit of returning to a topic, bolsters this interpretation
at *Paradise Lost* VI. 250 ff. and 317–18. But (as Lionel Trilling once
remarked to me) "engine" gives pause. "Engine" makes the modern reader
think only of a battery engine or a machine with moving parts. While a
sword can be an "engine" under both definitions 5a and 10 under *engine*
in the *OED*, and while I once offered some illustrative quotations—from
the seventeenth century to the nineteenth—of old usage, only now have I
come upon, in Sir Walter Scott's *The Talisman* (1825), a specific reference
to a "two-handed sword" as an "engine."

It occurs in the penultimate chapter, XXVII, where Richard Coeur
de Lion and Saladin give a friendly demonstration of what the weapon of
each can do.

> It was Richard's two-handed sword that chiefly attracted the
> attention of the Saracen, a broad straight blade, the seemingly
> unwieldy length of which extended well-nigh from the shoulder to
> the heel of the warrior.

The English king accepts an invitation to show what his mighty arm and
sword can achieve—against a steel mace.

> The glittering broadsword, wielded by both his hands, arose aloft to
> the King's left shoulder, circled round his head, descended with the
> sway of some terrific engine, and the bar of iron rolled on the
> ground in two pieces, as a woodsman would sever a sapling with a
> hedging-bill.

We recall not only the terrific threat in "Lycidas," but "the sword of
Michael...with huge two-handed sway / Brandished aloft the horrid edge
came down" against Satan's shield (*PL* VI. 250 ff.), especially as the
situation in the novel involves a rivalry between a Christian and a
nonbeliever. The sword interpretation of the mysterious engine in
"Lycidas" dated from Warburton in Warton in the eighteenth century. We
may speculate that Scott followed it in every sense of the word.

SHAKESPEARE'S EMILIA AND MILTON'S:
THE PARAMETERS OF RESEARCH

"In the old age black was not counted fair," acknowledged Shakespeare in Sonnet CXXVII. It may be a literally incredible coincidence that the two greatest English poets wrote sonnets to a Dark Lady whose name was Emilia. Presumably it was not the same Emilia: unless Milton was drawn to a woman who in 1630 was sixty–one. But they may have been related––the name was very rare in England––and what more plausible than that the same family repeated the name? What has turned up of the first Emilia is negative: she had a son, Henry, and her grandchildren were Henry and Mary.[1]

A.L. Rowse's theory, presented in 1973[2] with characteristic flourish and self–confidence, has been much doubted. Let S. Schoenbaum epitomize the skepticism: "Dr. Rowse believes that Emilia Bassano, the natural daughter of Baptist, was the dark seductress of the *Sonnets*. Possibly––but the key word in the manuscript describing her was not, as first reported, brown, but brave. It is useful for a Dark Lady to be demonstrably dark."[3] Schoenbaum also notes that Rowse "silently revises his account" only a few months after publishing it.[4] After the doubts and corrections what is left? what George Steiner called "a beguiling possibility."[5]

John S. Smart's 1913 identification[6] of the Christian name of Milton's poetical mistress has also met with some opposition. Smart, it will be recalled, made an inference from the first two lines of the first Italian sonnet: "Donna leggiadra, il cul bel nome onora / L'erbosa val di Reno e il nobil varco." "The flowery vale of Reno" is the region known since Roman times as Emilia (referred to, indeed, in *Paradise Regained* IV, 69) and "the famous ford" is the Rubicon. (I might add, for the fun of it, that one town in the region is Bazzono.) Other Renaissance poets encoded or played on their mistresses' names in their sonnets. Smart even found (143) in "Gandolfo Porrino, a poet of minor note" Milton's words "il cui bel nome onora" (a discovery that the *Variorum Commentary on the Italian Poems* neglects to record), where "the name disclosed by the poet is *Lucia,* or *Light*." In 1954 I suggested that Milton had enshrined the etymology of Katherine, "pure," in his sonnet on his deceased wife.[7] Sonnet X ends with "honoured Margaret," which Anna K. Nardo in 1979[8] found in context to be hinting at the etymology of that name, *pearl* (after the examples of Tasso and Claudio Tolomei).

E.A.J. Honigmann[9] objected that Smart should have printed, not "Reno," but "Rheno," the reading of the editions of 1645 and 1673. This suggests, he said, "the Rhine rather than the insignificant Reno," and Frankfurt is a famous ford in the Rhineland, though not on the Rhine. One must reply that the orthographical variant is of no consequence--"Rheno" may be either Reno or Rhine--but if Milton had been addressing a Rhinemaiden we should have expected his "lingua ignota e strana" ("Canzone," 3) to be German. Equally unlikely, it seems to me, is John T. Shawcross's turning Milton's lady into an abstraction, a "personification representing the inspiration through which man can raise earthly beauty and love to emulate heavenly beauty and love."[10] As *A Milton Encyclopedia*[11] mildly comments, "not all will agree." This is not the Milton I know through his other works. He did not have an allegoric frame of mind. Even Spenser's *Amoretti* are addressed to a real woman.

The generality of editors and commentators, including Shawcross himself in his 1971 edition of the *Complete Poetry*, accept Smart's identification. The deficiency is, of course, that we do not have a last name for her. Rowse, when he went on to do *Milton the Puritan,*[12] showed surprisingly little interest in *this* problem, saying merely:

> Nothing distracted him, as he said, from his aim. Certainly not the mere glimpse of a dark-eyed Italian girl, of rare name Emilia--, about whom he wrote in his Italian sonnets. (Shakespeare's Dark Lady, another Emilia, *née* Bassano, Mrs. Lanier, was still alive, in her sixties; her husband's cousin, Nicholas Lanier, was a distinguished musician and connoisseur, agent for the King in building up his unparalleled collection of pictures.)

By normal usage, "the rare name" applies to the blank that Rowse does not fill in. Well, what is so rare as no name at all? I should have expected Rowse to speculate on a connection with the numerous tribe of Bassanos in England, of which the *New Grove Dictionary of Music and Musicians* (1980) says, "it is impossible to establish their genealogy or to trace the careers of individual members."

In his researches did Rowse ever come upon another Emilia? Donald Dorian may or may not have. *The English Diodatis*[13] has a tantalizing note: "In examining lists totalling many thousand names for information on the Diodati circle, I have noticed it [Emilia] only once." Once may be enough. What was that once? Maybe it was Rowse's long-lived Emilia again: she died in 1645 at age seventy–six.[14] Rowse boasted, "nothing whatever has appeared about her in print,"[15] not knowing that Smart had already printed her name in 1913 as part of his quest for Milton's mistress.[16]

Surely Ernest Brennecke, Jr. in his *John Milton the Elder and His Music*[17] was being plausible when he remarked:

> Emilia's actual identity has thus far eluded investigators [how many have there been?], but it seems reasonable to suppose that this dark lady of Milton's sonnets was a daughter of one of the many professional Italian musicians with whom the Lawes brothers, the Miltons, and the Diodatis were consorting at the time. Her last name may have been Ferrabosco, Bassano, Lupo, or Galliardello [Nicholas Lanier's mother was a Galliardello]––and her rather bewitching personality throws a romantic and enigmatic aura over our picture of the musical diversions at Bread Street.

Leafing through the standard works, Grove's *Dictionary*, the *DNB*, William Woodfill's *Musicians in English Society from Elizabeth to Charles I* (Princeton University Press, 1953), one has to be impressed what a man's world it was. Wives and mothers and sisters and daughters are not mentioned (outside the nobility). Sons seem simply to spring from the head of the father. No women are in the King's Musick. The discrimination continues in Pepys' *Diary*, where there are scores of "Mrs." without first name. There is, for relevant instance, Mrs. Ferrabosco, descended, probably, from the famous Alphonso (died 1628). Like Shakespeare and Milton, Pepys had no prejudice against "black": "Anon comes the Duchesse [of Newcastle] with her women attending her; among others the Ferabosco, of whom so much talk is that her lady would bid her show her face and kill the gallants. She is indeed black, and hath good black little eyes, but otherwise but a very ordinary woman I do think, but they say sings well." (May 30, 1667, around the time *Paradise Lost* was being licensed.)

In *Shakespeare the Man* Rowse decided that the Christian name of Emilia's husband must have been William because of Shakespeare's "Will" sonnets.[18] Later he found out that the name was Alfonso,[19] but this apparently bothered him no more than the misreading of "brave" as "brown."[20] I should like Milton's lady to turn out to be Emilia Varco, capitalizing "il nobil varco" and connecting with *I Sonetti* of Benedetto Varchi that Milton owned and annotated.[21] Did not Parker suggest, "Perhaps Emilia's last name is also hidden in the sonnets?"[22] The unusual tercets in three of them have a rhyme–scheme found in Varchi.[23] Sergio Baldi's "Poesie Italiane di Milton"[24] takes occasion to cite this Florentine often. In his key opening lines Milton was imitating Varchi's Sonnets XLII and DVI:

Vezzoso fonte [an affluent of the Arno],
    che tra mille honori
Di rose, e gigli molle argento scendi,
E del ginebro il tuo bel nome prendi,
Vincino a lei che si chiamò da fiori...

Donna, che (come chiaro a ciascun mostra
Il nome, l'opre più) l'alma del uero
Cibo nodrite...   [Caterina Cibo][25]

With such precedent, look, then, at line 5 of Milton's first sonnet, "Che dolcemente mostrasi": does one have to be a Baconian to find hidden there "Benedetto"?

In any case the name should be Italian. All that remains is to find it! It should not be beyond hope that someone in a better position than I to do the requisite research, in manuscripts, genealogies, wills, parish registers––or someone with just a bit of serendipitous luck––can give a body and a name to the "Donna leggiadra" who sang so enchantingly. And she would have to be more respectable than that other Emilia––relative or not––of deplorable birth and morals.[26]

But reform can come, as we see with her namesake in *Othello*, a reform that enables us to end on a poetic chord. The first Emilia, in 1611, at forty-two, turned pious and published––a rare thing for a woman to do––a book, a volume of religious verse (this was the year of the King James Bible), in which––another rare thing––she digressed into an "Eves Apologie." There is no doubting the seriousness and sufficient learning of *Salve Deus Rex Ivdaeorvm* (the title came to her in a dream) "Written by Mistris *Aemilia Lanyer*, Wife to Captaine *Alfonso Lanyer*, Seruant to the Kings Majestie."[27] "Vouchsafe to view that which is seldome seene, / A Womans writing of divinest things" (41). She can sound like early, very early, Milton:

Yet if he please t'illuminate my Spirit,
And give me Wisdom from his holy Hill,
That I may Write part of his glorious Merit,
If he vouchsafe to guide my Hand and Quill,
To shew his Death, by which we doe inherit
Those endlesse Joyes that all our hearts doe fill;
Then will I tell of that sad black fac'd Night
Whose mourning Mantle covered Heavenly light. (89)

Milton began a stanza on daybreak, "So when the sun in bed" ("On the Morning of Christ's Nativity," 229). Emilia starts one of her stanzas, "Come like the morning Sunne new out of bed" (52). "Heavens Eternall

King" is a phrase common to both (139; Nativity Hymn, 2). So is "eternall blisse" (87; *PL* 12. 551). With a common source in Scripture, Milton wrote, "How oft amidst / Thick clouds and dark doth heav'n's all-ruling Sire / Choose to reside" (PL 2. 263–5), while Emilia puts it briefly, "And cloudes of darknesse compasse him about" (82). Not in Scripture, however, is this proto-feminist's spirited defence of Eve against Adam, well summarized in one line: "Her fault though great, yet hee was most too blame" (103). Milton, aged three in 1611, might already have had something to say about that!

NOTES

1. A.L. Rowse, *Simon Forman: Sex and Society in Shakespeare's Age* (London: Weidenfeld and Nicolson, 1974): 99, 116.
2. Rowse, *Shakespeare the Man* (New York: Harper): 87–113; *Shakespeare's Sonnets: The Problems Solved*, xxvii–xlv.
3. Schoenbaum, *William Shakespeare: A Documentary Life* (New York: Oxford University Press, 1975): 127.
4. *Ibid.*, n. 3. The reference is to *Simon Forman*. A damaging review appeared in *TLS*, June 7, 1974, 604.
5. Steiner, "Portrait of a Lady," *The New Yorker*, March 18, 1974, 148 (142–50).
6. Best known through Smart's edition of *The Sonnets of Milton* (Glasgow: Maclehose, Jackson, 1921): 137–44. But it should not be stated, "Even the riddled name of Emilia (in the opening lines of the first sonnet) was not discovered until 1921." W.R. Parker, *Milton: A Biography* (Oxford, 1968): 78. Smart put forth his discovery in "The Italian Singer in Milton's Sonnets," *The Musical Antiquary*, 4 (1912–13): 91–97, an article Parker knew (929, n. 35), although it is not in David H. Stevens, *Reference Guide to Milton from 1800 to the Present Day* (Chicago: University of Chicago Press, 1930). Harris F. Fletcher listed it, *Contributions to a Milton Bibliography 1800–1930* (Urbana: University of Illinois Press, 1930): 106, but also was inaccurate in saying: "Material later incorporated in Smart's volume on the sonnets." Only in the article does Smart give us the now startling coincidence that he came upon documentary evidence of the existence in 1576 of Emilia Bassano (without connecting her––the link there was Simon Forman––with Shakespeare).
7. Le Comte, "The Veiled Face of Milton's Wife," *N & Q*, n.s., I, 245–46.
8. Nardo, *Milton's Sonnets and the Ideal Community* (Lincoln: University of Nebraska Press): 52–53, 187–90.
9. Ed., *Milton's Sonnets* (London: Macmillan, 1966): 80, n. 1.
10. Shawcross, "Milton's Italian Poems: An Interpretation," *University of Windsor Review*, 3 (1967), 33 (27–33).
11. Eds., William B. Hunter, Jr. et al. (Lewisburg: Bucknell University Press, 1980), 8, 20 (article by James Dale).
12. (London: Macmillan, 1977): 28. For another strange indifference, "there is, very curiously, not a single allusion to Bassanio [of *The Merchant of Venice*] or to the possible connection between his name and that of the Bassano–Bassanye family in either *Shakespeare the Man* or *Shakespeare's Sonnets: The Problems Solved*." Hugh Maclean, "Bassanio's Name and Nature," *Names*, 25

(1977), 58 (55–62). And what about Forman as the model for Prospero in *The Tempest*? I filled that speculative gap with "A Postscript" to my *Poets' Riddles: Essays in Seventeenth–Century Explication* (Port Washington, N.Y.: Kennikat Press, 1975): 183–84.

13. (New Brunswick: Rutgers University Press, 1950): 265, n. 46.
14. Rowse, ed., *The Poems of Shakespeare's Dark Lady: "Salve Deus Rex Judaeorum"* by *Emilia Lanier* (New York: Clarkson N. Potter, 1979): 37.
15. *Shakespeare the Man*, 105; cf. *Shakespeare's Sonnets*, xliv.
16. "The Italian Singer in Milton's Sonnets," 95.
17. (New York: Columbia University Press, 1938): 119.
18. *Shakespeare the Man*, 93–94, 105–06, 109–10, 112; cf. *Shakespeare's Sonnets*, 281, 283, xxxvii–viii.
19. *Simon Forman*, by implication on 116; stated outright only in the Index under "Lanier," 312.
20. Rowse was still defying his critics in 1982: "Emilia Bassano, the half–Italian musical lady, who was unanswerably the Dark Lady of the sonnets," a curious adverb considering how much Rowse has been answered. Rowse, "Following the Footsteps of the Bard," Travel Section, *The New York Sunday Times*, November 28, 1982, 14.
21. See Maurice Kelley, "Milton's Dante–Della Casa–Varchi Volume," *Bulletin of the New York Public Library*, 66 (1962), 499–504.
22. *Milton*, 744.
23. See J.E. Shaw and A. Bartlett Giamatti, eds., *A Variorum Commentary on the Italian Poems* (New York: Columbia University Press, 1970): 369.
24. *Studi secenteschi*, VII (1966), "Bibliotéca dell' Archivum Romanicum," vol. 90, 103–30.
25. Baldi, 116.
26. A biographer who is also a novelist imagines someone sorting through Milton's papers after his death, finding "A billet–doux signed `Emilia'"––and burning it!. A.N. Wilson, *The Life of John Milton* (Oxford: Oxford University Press, 1983), 254.
27. I quote from Rowse's edition (note 14 above), with page numbers in parenthesis. For a bibliographical description see Barbara K. Lewalski, "Of God and Good Women: The Poems of Aemilia Lanyer," in *Silent but for the Word*, ed., Margaret Hannay (Kent State Press, 1985), 203–24. The handicaps are set forth by Elaine V. Beilin, *Redeeming Eve: Women Writers of the English Renaissance* (Princeton University Press, 1987). Before her current rediscovery I had occasion to cite Lady Mary Wroth in *The Notorious Lady Essex* (New York: Dial Press, 1969), 213. Lanier won entrance to the 5th ed. of *The Oxford Companion to English*

Literature, ed., Margaret Drabble (Oxford: Oxford University Press, 1985), 549.

THE *INDEX* TO THE COLUMBIA MILTON:
ITS VIRTUES AND DEFECTS

Recently I needed the text of Tennyson's lines on Milton. My *Milton Dictionary* (1961)[1] says that the title is "Milton." Taking down from my shelf the standard Macmillan one–volume *Works of Tennyson* (1913), I looked in the Index of Titles. No "Milton," no "On Milton." Would it be necessary to riffle through 878 pages? I turned to the index to W.R. Parker's biography of Milton (Oxford: Oxford University Press, 1968), a marvel of comprehensiveness, but for once it let me down. Next I tried the index (London: Macmillan, 1894) to David Masson's six–volume biography and was referred to 6, 555, where the lines are quoted. But no title is given. Masson just calls it a "Horatian ode." Nothing of the sort is listed in the Macmillan Tennyson. Staring at Masson's quotation, "O mighty–mouth'd inventor of harmonies," etc., I progressed to the Macmillan Index to the First Lines and was enabled to find the poem on page 237. It is indeed headed "MILTON" and underneath that, "Alcaics." But "Alcaics" is not in the Index of Titles either. The only title given countenance is the group title, "In Quantity." Who would ever have threaded that maze to Tennyson's once–famous lines?

Inadequate indexes can be worse than none because they mislead. I had wondered whether, for some reason of copyright or fragmentariness, my old Tennyson did not include the verses. Actually a true scholar might be defined as one who never trusts, or even uses, an index––but reads right through, whatever it is. But the average frail Miltonist will rejoice in the proliferation of, and progress in, reference books pertaining to his learned author, right up to the *Milton Encyclopedia* and *its* Index (Lewisburg: Bucknell University Press, 1984). Whatever may be said about progress in literary criticism (*is* there?), much instant help to learning "Hath been achieved of merit" (*Paradise Lost* 2. 21).

Compare the indexes to the two most comprehensive biographies, aforementioned. In number of pages they are close––Masson's 242 double–columned pages versus Parker's 275. But the "three members of my own household" who compiled Masson's index decided not to include his footnotes. Thus hundreds of names are missing, names important to the bibliography of Milton and to 17th–century history. Anthony Wood, for instance, is cited only for his three appearances in the text, never as a source (as at 6, 213).

Parker goes to the opposite extreme of including what he has not mentioned. As he says (1215), "This index includes almost all the *names* mentioned and many of the *subjects* discussed in both text and notes, the more important ones indicated by bold–face type. It includes much besides, in an effort to be useful to the curious reader and to future investigators of Milton's biography." There are, for example, three Nelsons: the contemporary scholars James G. and Lowry, Jr., each cited once, and, sandwiched in between, "Jeremiah, stud. Christ's 1626 (d. 1685)"––whose only existence in Parker's 1489 pages is in this entry. Joseph Frank is listed for two books, not cited. Unlike the *Milton Encyclopedia*, which omits living Miltonists, this index has sometimes overgenerous listings (as in mentioning the title of my first book, although it is not about Milton).

The topic entries compete with such books as William J. Grace's *Ideas in Milton* (Notre Dame, 1968) and Ruth Mohl's *John Milton and His Commonplace Book* (New York: Frederick Ungar, 1969) and William C. Johnson's *Milton Criticism: A Subject Index* (Kent: Dawson, 1978). Under "freedom" we are referred to "liberty" also––and vice versa (for "free will, *see* freedom"). Interested in "loneliness"?––it is there (of which more anon). There are surprisingly copious bibliographies: for Tennyson six articles or books, for "Lycidas" numerous editions followed by numerous translations. One is overwhelmed by such meticulous bounty. It goes far beyond a biographer's duty, was the cause of long delay in publication and putatively Parker's last heart attack. I cannot think of anything missing, except a listing of all the contributors to *Justa Edovardo King*.

Parker's Index, then, is one of the 20th–century monuments. Before going to another, the Columbia Milton Index, which is, for one thing, a partial concordance to the poetry, a word might appropriately be said about the history of Milton concordances, again a story of progress.[2] Once should be enough for a concordance, but that is not the way it has worked out. In the beginning was the Verbal Index––to *Paradise Lost* only, as compiled by Thomas Coxeter and published in 1741. This was appended to Thomas Newton's variorum editions of the latter half of the 18th century (1749 on). Its apotheosis was the computer–based *Concordance* to the 1674 poem produced by Gladys W. Hudson (Detroit: Gale, 1970). Newton added to the Verbal Index an interesting name–and–topic index (dating back to Thomas Tickell, 1720) that included SIMILES. The first edition of Henry John Todd's six–volume variorum (London: J. Johnson, etc., 1801) ended with a "Glossarial Index of Words, Phrases, Customs, and Persons, Explained or Mentioned in the Notes." The final growth of this (18 pages) would be Laura E. Lockwood's *Lexicon to the English Poetical Works of John Milton* (New York: Macmillan, 1907). For his second edition, 1809, Todd outdid Newton with a Verbal Index to all the poems, including the foreign-language poems. This apparatus in Volume I--406 unnumbered pages--was also published in the same year as a separate volume as part of *Some Account of the Life and Writings*. Todd remarked, forebodingly (vi), "It is not pretended, that in such a multiplicity of references the reader might seek in vain for errours. The vigilance of the nicest eye, it will be allowed, may, in attending to a work of this kind, be sometimes deceived." Todd dropped his "laborious" compilation from subsequent editions, but not because Charles Dexter Cleveland complained it had 3362 mistakes.[3] Cleveland put out in 1867 what he entitled *A Complete Concordance*, but "it was merely a verbal index."[4] The first two true concordances were both dated, strange to say, from Madras. Copyists and compositors with too little English spoiled the two-volume effort (barely circulated) by Guy Lushington Prendergast of 1857-59.

What long remained the standard *Concordance* came posthumously from John Bradshaw (a name Milton honored!) in 1894 (London: Sonnenschein). He did not cope with original spellings and textual variations (such as in the manuscript of "Lycidas"), as does what might be called that last word, the computer-generated *Concordance to Milton's English Poetry* (including the psalm translations and translations in the prose) by William Ingram and Kathleen Swaim (Oxford: Oxford University Press, 1972).

In the 1930's there was, of course, no computer to aid Frank Allen Patterson, general editor of what remains the only edition of Milton's complete works, in the indexing enterprise that was to be the capstone to those 18 volumes in 21. *An Index to the Columbia Edition of the Works of John Milton* (2 vols., 1940) was eight years in the making. In the last two and a half Patterson needed--and received--fresh blood in the form of the young French Rowe Fogle.

I knew them both. Fogle was my teacher for a day, taking over graduate class in Patterson's absence. Patterson was a man exhausted, a very tired teacher. A fellow student in the pre-doctoral seminar, Elizabeth Hardwick, was so bored she moved on to a different career. I was told Patterson had once had energy. The last of it had gone into the "two large volumes containing more than 170,000 entries" (ix)--on 2141 pages. He saw me through my doctor's oral, sold me his Pollard and Redgrave *Short-Title Catalogue*, and retired to Leonia, New Jersey, where he died not many months later (in 1944). William Haller of Barnard College (with whom Patterson was not on speaking terms) succeeded to his courses.

Patterson was, I believe, of the evangelical persuasion. He baited nuns and Catholic priests in his classes, like a latter-day Milton. One sentence in his preface has church-like echoes: "I have searched the

Scriptures both daily and diligently, but make no claim to entire success" (vi). Patterson's devotion to Milton was a form of piety.

Patterson commenced work on the *Index* in 1932, before volumes IX–XVIII of the Columbia edition were even out. But he did a trial run in *The Student's Milton* as revised in 1933 (New York: Crofts) (still the most Milton ever packed into one volume), with its 37–page Glossary, where, besides names, one could look up unusual words, or unusual usages. There were, besides, Patterson's notes. For Satan's "If counsels different" (*PL* 1. 636) I gave Patterson credit in my *Dictionary of Puns in Milton's English Poetry* (New York: Columbia University Press, 1981) for two of four possible definitions: "(1) different from what they should have been; (2) different from those held by others" (Patterson's "Notes on the Poetry," 79).

Actually there is no *different* in the *Index*, which slights modifiers and verbs in favor of nouns. This is consonant with the goal to be a literal index to Milton's ideas. What we have, primarily, is a selective concordance of Milton's words or those of that edition's translators. Suppose you wish to locate "I cannot praise a fugitive and cloistered virtue, unexercised and unbreathed, that never sallies out and sees her adversary." This can be found under fugitive, cloistered, virtue, unexercised, sallies, adversary. Who will miss *unbreathed*? As for *see* and *sees*, there is only one verb entry (*PL* 5. 411), the others being nouns ("the see of Canterbury," etc.). William Kerrigan has lately remarked on "the many representations of intrusive and aggressive seeing" in *Paradise Lost*,[5] but that is a matter of (Freudian) interpretation, to be checked, if you like, with a complete concordance to the poetry. As long as we have the final efficiency of Ingram and Swaim, we need not care what the Patterson *Index* does or does not do with the English poetry––and for the foreign language poems there has been since 1923 Lane Cooper, *A Concordance of the Latin, Greek, and Italian Poems of John Milton* (Halle: Max Niemeyer).

As it happens, a goodly number of respected scholars have printed in the *Areopagitica* passage, instead of "sees her adversary," "seeks her adversary."[6] You might wonder whether Milton said something comparable elsewhere. The scholars' plausible mistake might be indicative of a misprint in the original text. But there is no *seek(s)* in the *Index*, nor is there a pertinent *adversary*. Try a synonym. *Enemy*? A persistent seeker will be led to "encounter a real enemy" ("verum hostem petere") in *Pro Se Defensio* (9, 224–5), as the end of a sentence with other parallels to the *Areopagitica* one. The Yale Milton translation has, indeed, "seek a real enemy."

If you do not know where "closing up truth to truth" (4, 339) occurs, you will be led an unmerry chase through columns and columns of "Truth" because there is no entry for *closing*. On the other hand, Patterson has *acuminating* because it belongs to the category of peculiar, along with the verb *amate*. *Amerced* is given, but *amerce* is not: "why in such a case they may not finally amerce him with the loss of his Kingdom" (5, 5?). The *Index* silently instructs us that "adagies" means *adages* (3, 286). It is not an old spelling index, and that can lead to rather wide gaps. The disputed word in *Areopagitica*, "muing" (4, 344), you will find it only under *mewing*. I recall a writer on Marvell's "The Nymph Complaining" who got mixed up on the difference between a fawn and a faun. The same misfortune overtakes the *Index* when it fails to modernize "Fawn" in *Paradise Regained* (2. 191) as *Faun*. At least it has a correct entry for *fawns* (*PL* 4. 404), which the Swaim *Concordance* does not. Patterson gives "farding" as *farthing*. "Incompetible" (3, 84) you will not find under *incompatible*, for neither is there.

The list of "unusual, obsolete" (ix) words included is long.[7] My list of those omitted is, naturally, shorter; I find no rationale behind it. I suppose *Apeirokalia* (3, 301) was left out because it is printed in Greek letters. Indeed it proved so intimidating that the noun "Greek" which immediately precedes it was also bypassed, contrary to the rules that had been set. Greek and Latin were not Professor Patterson's strong point. Professor Moses Hadas of the classics department at Columbia told me he was enlisted to measure off the facing pages of some of the Latin prose and its translation. Not looking at Milton's Latin forms of names has resulted in some deficiencies, as we shall see.

Replaceable though it is as a guide to the poetry, it is surprising that among the missing are such distinctive words as *beldam, crisped, ellops, grunsel, gurge, haut, hist, irriguous, mickle, purfled, rathe, recure, sculls, spets, subducting, unexempt, unhide-bound*. *Terf(e)* (meaning turf) occurs four times in the poetry, but is found under neither spelling. In the area of the misleading is entering *unweeting* as a single occurrence (*PR* 1. 126), when there are four others (*PL* 10. 335, 916; *Comus* 539; "Fair Infant," 23), not to mention *unweetingly* (*SA* 1680). For the English prose you will not find *bankets* (3, 206), *bates* (5, 269), *beteemed* (3, 159), *cantle* (3, 440), *chanonies* (3, 73), *coulters* (4, 328), *disple* (3, 36), *dorre* (3, 310), *glouting* (3, 4), *smach* (3, 353), *toling* (3, 289). For Gower's *Confessio Amantis* as quoted in *An Apology for Smectymnuus* (3, 360) you will look in vain for *left* meaning sky, and *yafe* and *yeft*. In the same pamphlet we do have *chase*: "I am like to chase him into some good knowledge" (3, 292); the plausible reading of some copies, *chafe*, could not be indexed because it was not noted in the Columbia edition.[8]

Before going on to proper names, let us make a small test of topics, ("boundless the deep" here). Consider "In darkness, and with dangers compast round, / And solitude" (*PL* 7. 27–8). I would go along with the *Index*: "In darkness" is a reference to Milton's—or, as it is currently fashionable to say, the narrator's, or the persona's—*blindness*, though it could be argued that the poet has more in mind night dangers, "*Bacchus* and his revellers" (33), drunken carousers in the London streets not unlike those the Lady of *Comus* encountered in a dark wood. You will not, however, find any of this passage under *Cavaliers*. Is not *solitude* (duly entered) a synonym for *loneliness*, which the *Index* confines to the word's appearances in the divorce tracts? True, the poet immediately issues a denial, "yet not alone, while thou / Visit'st," etc., but the subject has been raised. Parker's Index leads us to interpretations--"*Lycidas* was an expression of loneliness" (188)--that we cannot expect of a concordance. Parker also leads us (180) to that poignant "lonely in a crowd" letter to Carlo Dati (12, 46) that we can find in Patterson only under the literal *solitude*. Advice to user: try synonyms, find topics. Whereas Milton's Latin is "solitudine," Parker, differing from Columbia (Masson) and Yale (Turner) and Shawcross, translates "loneliness" (311), as did Phyliss Tillyard.[9] But he indexes *PL* 7. 28 (the whole passage is quoted on page 587) under *solitude*, not loneliness.

Oddly enough, where Milton wrote "Egyptian tyranny" in *The Reason of Church-Government* (3, 222), Patterson, under "Egyptian," has "E. bondage of prelacy" (though *tyranny* is correctly indexed). Similarly, "trivial and various pretences" (5, 126) is altered to "trivial and frivolous" under *pretences*. "*Divide* and conquer": you are led to think Milton used that expression five times. He never used it at all. He *was* rather given to picturing *necks* in subjection. The *Index* bypasses the earliest case, "In Quintum Novembris," 111, where none of the vivid words of the Charles Knapp translation is entered: "trample with godless feet your holy neck" (1, 245).

Many, perhaps most, will use the *Index* only for proper names. It is important that none be missing. Imagine all the discussions with the key statement, "Milton never mentions------." The goal has to be, and was, total inclusion. Did any names slip through the wide-flung net? Moreover, are there names Milton is indexed as mentioning that he did not in fact mention? The answer to both questions is yes.

You will not find the first occurrence of *Dan* in *Samson Agonistes* (332). You will not find certain names that are in the Columbia text of the poetry--the text that is supposed to be indexed--unless you figure out their modern equivalents (on which no guidance is given), which alone are entered. You read "Darwen stream," Sonnet XVI. 7 (I, 65): to be found only under *Derwent*. "*Rhene* or the Danaw," *PL* 1. 353 (2, 21): not there, see *Rhine, Danube*. It is as if the editor really does not believe in the texts in their original form that he set out so scrupulously to present. He looks back to the modernized prose of *The Student's Milton* and to modernized texts of the poetry. That is what the *Index* is telling us he believes in. It was practical to modernize, but not to neglect the old. We have to have full accounting, "Piemont" (1, 66) as well as *Piedmont*. What about Milton's own variant, *Tesiphon* (*PR* 3. 292) and *Ctesiphon* (300), the same city? Both should have been indexed under both spellings, but you will not discover the former under the latter, nor the latter under the former.

The Glossary to *The Student's Milton*, while omitting Tesiphon, at least gives both references under Ctesiphon. Patterson should have entered all variants of names--which would mostly consist of Milton's and the modern--just as, for the texts, "the several editors attempt to furnish full textual information" (1, 7) (however inadequate later editors, such as Harris Fletcher, found *that* effort) (then Parker found Fletcher inadequate: scholarship is a succession of complaints!).[10] Nor is a questionable practice carried out uniformly. Did Milton ever refer to Rhadamanthus? The *Index* is negative, unless you check (but who would?) *Radamanthus* (4, 305). But "Savenarola" (3, 125) or "Savanaruola" (18, 165) is corrected.

The Latin poetry was regularly not looked at, only the translation. There is no entry for Mareotis ("In Quintum Novembris," 171) because the translator has "Maeotis" (1, 249). There has been conjecture of a misprint,[11] but Lake Mareotis is not Lake Maeotis, and a silent substitution is improper. Neither facing page gives warrant for Japetus, instead of Iapetus, in "In Obitum Procancellarii Medici," 4 (1, 232–3). Milton did not name "Pan" in 'Epitaphium Damonis," 169: the translator's "Pan's pipe" for "fistula" misled and should at most have been "panpipe" (1, 313). Elegia I. 3 has Deva (not *Dee*) as surely as "Lycidas," 55: an interesting Latin–to–English connection has gone downstream. "Eolus" is not found in dictionaries, or in Milton, or in his translator (El. IV. 6: "Æolon"). Æoliades is found in Milton (El. VI. 51) but not in the *Index*. For Pyrenen (El. V. 10), see Pirene, for Tyro (12, 220), see Tiro, for Mavors ("Naturam non Pati Senium," 40), see Mars, for Asopus ("In Quintum Novembris," 66), see Æsopus (not to be confused with Aesop), for Corus ("Naturam," 53), see Caurus, for Jögernen ("Epitaphium Damonis," 166), see Igraine, for Pausilipi ("Ad Leonoram Romae Canentem" 3.6), see Posilipo. (For "Poole," the Cardinal, 4, 136, see Pole.) "Hours (Horae), daughters of Themis and of Jove" ("In Obitum Praesulis Eliensis," 39–40; 1, 256–7) should have been entered as a name; there is no entry at all. Did Milton ever refer to Tasso by his first name ("Torquatum," "Ad Leonoram" 2. 1)? You will not find out by looking it up.

It is assumed now, it was assumed fifty years ago, that no one is left who would look at, much less read, Milton's Latin. We have the phenomenon of eight portly volumes coming out, edited by some of the leading scholars of our day, entitled *Complete Prose Works of John Milton*--and what is meant is translations. And translations were what Patterson was indexing too. At the risk of being accused of biting the hand that fed me--the *Index* was indispensable to my own two first books on Milton and I duly expressed my debt therein--I am entering a word, or many words, of caution to the users of that stupendous key. Some policies were not carried out in all detail, there were naturally some errors (including misprints),[12] and some policies I think wrong. Wrong, I think, was not having references (which would be cross-references) to Latin place names. Consider "ad Riphæos ultimos" in *Defensio Prima* (7, 284). This will not be found, except as the dubious translation "to utmost Siberia" (7, 285). Yale (4, 430) also gives Siberia, which, however, is not named as the equivalent in Allan H. Gilbert's *A Geographical Dictionary of Milton* (Ithaca: Cornell University Press, 1919) or the *Oxford Classical Dictionary* (eds., N.G.L. Hammond and H.H. Scullard, 2nd ed., 1970)--or even in Milton's account of the Riphaean Mountains in *A Brief History of Moscovia* (10, 333). It may do, at least as metaphor, but the real pity is that where Milton has two--even three (18, 331)--references to the same place, one falls through the net.

The same holds true for two references to the same personage, the daughter of Pandrasus, a legendary king of Greece. She is "Innogen" in the *History of Britain* (10, 10) (as in the new Oxford *Cymbeline*). The policy of modernizing should have made the transformation "Inogen." But that is missing even for Milton's prior reference "Inogeniae" ("Epitaphium Damonis," 163)--because the translator has "Imogene."

An index that was so careful as to list the unnamed Memnon of "In Quintum Novembris," 135, and the unnamed Deborah of 7, 60-61 (interpolations by the translators), should also have added to "Hercules" the poetical references (major) to Alcides. By the time the compiler reached "W" there was, doubtless, such weariness that *Wager* through *Wagons* are out of alphabetical order. Disconcerting is to suffer a miscopying or misprint, as "Thrasbylus" for "Thrasybulus"--and then put the error in correct alphabetical order. I thought Alciat(i) (4, 229) was totally missing until I came upon it as "Aliciat." Missing are Aërians (5, 232; *not* the same as *Arians*), Balaam (6, 50), Bosor (6, 329), Dillon (6, 245), Endymion (6, 337), Gerard (4, 222--not under *Du Haillan* either), Glaucus (7, 112), "Protector" (3, 8--to lead us to the unnamed but indexed *Somerset*). *Grandoes*--you might think it a mistake for "grandees," but "Granado's (5, 166)--modern, *grenades*--is meant. Where the translator has Cinnamus, Milton has the unlisted Sinnamus (12, 88-9). The cost of not giving the title page of the second edition of *The Ready and Easy Way* was to lose a quotation from *Juvenal*.

Some quick checking should have been done with names of persons. Christopher Hill would be pleased to think that Milton mentioned *Richard* Overton, but it was Colonel *Robert* Overton who was eulogized in *Defensio Secunda*. Pickering is not Benjamin but Gilbert, Gibson is James, not Thomas, Sydenham, William, not Cuthbert. "Lily, John"?--the author of *Euphues*? Milton's only Lily is William (4, 281), the first headmaster of St. Paul's School and author of the standard beginning textbook in Latin. Lysimachus should have been indexed (also) under Nicanor. Milton never names "Dobeneck," and it would have been better if the *Index* had not done so when it says: "Dobeneck, Johannes, D. recited by Cochlæus in his *Miscellanies* v 46 (T)." Dobeneck *is* Cochlæus.

The State Letters drafted in 1654 and 1655 to Charles X, the king of Sweden, are put under "Gustavus II. Adolphus," who fell at Lützen in 1632.

In light of later knowledge Fogle himself was able to make a correction to "David Blondel." The marginal "Blond." in the *History of Britain*, 10, 106 is not to that 17th–century Calvinist, but Flavius Blondus, the 15th–century Italian historian and archaeologist. Anticipated by Constance Nicholas's 1957 *Introduction and Notes to Milton's "History of Britain"* (Urbana: University of Illinois Press), 70, Fogle as the Yale editor, 5 (1971), 133, n. 19, got Milton's reference right.

Close student of the Bible though Patterson was, he confused the two Tamars and two Amaziahs. He mixes in the mother of Constantine with Helen of Troy. Needless to say, the intention was to have separate entries for different personages: this was not carried out for Aristobulus, Arsaces, Constantius, Crassus, Hermes, Herod, Pyrrhus, Saturninus, Scipio Africanus, Thomas Smith.

On the other hand, Prosper of Aquitane and Jonathan ben Uzziel are wrongly multiplied, while Theodosius II as mentioned at 7, 258, is put under Theodosius I. Perkin Warbeck: one entry (3, 102) is under Perkin, the second under Warbeck, and the second (appropriately) does not exist in Milton's Latin but is a figurative interpolation of the translator (7, 17). Milton wrote "Apollinarius" (4, 307); the *Index* has *Apollinaris*. We are given to understand that "In Obitum Praesulis Eliensis" mourns Nicholas Fenton (instead of Felton). The Brutus of 3, 92 (no note in Yale 1, 640), is not Marcus but Junius. The Curtius of 3, 220, was not Quintus.

A recent scholar followed Patterson into that last abyss. Jackson Campbell Boswell, *Milton's Library: A Catalogue of the Remains of John Milton's Library and an Annotated Reconstruction of Milton's Library and Ancillary Readings* (New York: Garland, 1975), lumps together the eponymous hero who saved Rome with Quintus Curtius Rufus, author of *De Rebus Gestis Alexandri Magni*. Patterson's next entry is for the latter (without the "Rufus") and is part of a further ambition, to go beyond being a concordance to give sources and hidden or implicit allusions, as pointed to by "the most important and notable commentaries, such as those by Newton, Todd, Warton, Keightley, Verity, and Browne" (vi) and such studies as Harris Fletcher's on Milton's use of the Bible and George C. Taylor's *Milton's Use of Du Bartas* (Cambridge, Mass.: Harvard University Press, 1934). At *Paradise Regained* 2. 196-8, "Remember that *Pellean* Conquerour, / A youth, how all the Beauties of the East / He slightly view'd, and slightly over-passed"; Newton gives a passage from "Quint. Curt. Lib. 3. cap. 9." It is pertinent. If the Malvezzi Marginalia are Milton's he referred to Curtius Rufus, and I do not see why the editor of the 1975 *Variorum* omitted this citation.[13] Boswell does correct "Clapmorius" to Clapmarius.

Boswell's listing of 1520 authors would of course have been of enormous help to Patterson (as Patterson was to Boswell). So would have the Columbia *Variorum Commentary on the Poems* and the Yale notes on the prose. For instance, another Chrysostom entry would have resulted at 18, 129, because Ruth Mohl in her copious notes for the Commonplace Book identified "Homil in Gen. 12" as by him (Yale, 1, 364). Actually James Holly Hanford had made this identification in 1921 in his seminal "The Chronology of Milton's Studies,"[14] but Patterson, having only one lifetime, could not roam among thousands of Milton studies but confined himself to what was handy, a few leading editions, a very few books.

It is now known that the reference in *Of Reformation* (3, 22) to Sandys is not to George but to his brother Sir Edwin (an understandable mistake, since both wrote travel books). Milton teased centuries of commentators when he wrote in *Areopagitica* (4, 313): "I name not him for posterities sake, whom *Harry* the 8. nam'd in merriment his Vicar of hell." Patterson entered the conjecture most popular, John *Skelton*, s.v. (but not in brackets elsewhere as would have been expected). As I wrote in the preface to my *Milton Dictionary*: "So far as Milton specialists are concerned, the correct identification...came with Merritt Hughes' edition of *Prose Selections*, 1947 (New York: Odyssey Press). But since 1932 all that the general reader had to do was look up `Vicar of Hell' in [Sir Paul Harvey's] *Oxford Companion [to English Literature]* and follow the cross-reference *Bryan*, where the identification is pinned down with all necessary despatch and authority."

In the other best-known tract, *Of Education*, I doubt if the following (4, 275) refers to Comenius: "I see those aims, those actions which have won you with me the esteem of a person sent hither by some good providence from a far country to be the occasion and the incitement of great good to this Island." Only on the next page do we get to Comenius (and this time the *Index* skips him): "to search what many modern *Janua's* and *Didactics* more than ever I shall read, have projected, my inclination leads me not" (276), a characteristic dismissal. The introduction to *Of Education* pays its respects to Hartlib. But at least Patterson serves to call attention to an ambiguity, where other commentators, such as the Yale, are silent.[15]

By expanding in the generous way that it does, the *Index* laid itself open to endless differences of scholarly opinion. Milton, unlike Sir Philip Sidney ("I never drank of Aganippe well," Sonnet LXXIV), never mentioned "Aganippe," taken as the allusion in the lovely passage, "Yet not the more / Cease I to wander where the Muses haunt / Cleer Spring" (*PL* 3. 28). Why may not the "Cleer Spring" be that other Heliconian spring, Hippocrene (higher on the mount and *the* spring for epic according to Propertius 3.3), or the Castalian, or the Pierian? Or unspecifiable? And if Sidney's famous opening line was supposed to be in the background, then the rule called for indexing him.

Citation of Aelian for the story of Alexander the Great sparing the house of Pindar (Sonnet VIII. 10)—a citation that dates back to Warton—has fallen by the wayside with modern annotators. Maybe it should be revived. The Bush *Variorum* gives eight alternatives to Keightley's *Telamon* as Hercules' "comes," El. VII. 40.

At times one cannot know which is a judgment call, which an oversight. Towards the bottom of the second column on page 430 it is startling to find a different David from the one that fills so many columns, to wit, David [Riccio], Mary Stuart's lover, whose name it would have been helpful to bracket. One misses "*conjugal* love" (4, 254) in *Colasterion*, perhaps even "*contrarieties* of minde" (4, 251). Considering the interest in the two-handed engine at the door, should we not have had the *ax* of *Pro Se Defensio* (9, 18-19), "even uplifted for the stroke"? What about El. I. 41-2 as a reference to Shakespeare's Romeo? One *has* to insist on *Boiardo* for *PR* 3. 337 ff.

Callimachus, *Hymn. in Jov.* 16 does not fit PL4. 703. Did a numeral—or much more—go wrong? Ancient texts are plagued with variations, as is well known. When Milton in his 1639 letter to the Vatican librarian Lucas Holstenius quotes Callimachus, "Feet to the earth still cling, while the head is touching Olympus," his penultimate word is *haptet'* (12, 44). The Loeb Library (Hymn VI, 58) has a different form of the verb, *hapsat'*. Epig. 24 on Cleombrotus is 25 in the Loeb Library edition; other editions drop No. 3 as spurious. Line *17* of *Hymn. in Jov.* does have Ladon and Erymanthus, like *Arcades*, 97, 100, if that is significant. With this as the influence, "Erymanth" is the river, not, as opted for by most editors, the mountain, and this would be strengthened by 18, 294, if only that annotation were in Milton's hand. But the Pindaric marginalia, including four references to Callimachus, have been argued not to be Milton's; in one fell sweep Kelley and Atkins in 1964[16] tossed out twenty-eight pages of the so-called *Works*. To return to Ladon and Erymanthus, six of Milton's names are collocated in Stephanus' dictionary, s.v. Arcadia, as Carey, following Starnes and Talbot, points out. I do not see how any part of *Hymn in Jov.* can be worked into any part of the epic, unless we compare the two stories of how was "watered all the ground" (7. 334).

We are invited to find the Bible all-pervasively. No doubt Joseph A. Wittreich, Jr., Apocalyptic speculator, would find the references to Revelation too few. *The Bible in Milton's Epics* by James H. Sims (Gainesville: University of Florida Press, 1962) constitutes a readable advance beyond Fletcher. Scholarship presses ever onward (when it does not go into reverse), and the serious user will struggle to take into account the contributions of the last fifty years. Looking up Shakespeare or Spenser,[17] for instance, one is off to a start with approximately two columns each (God has ninety), title by title, mostly echoes noted in editions of Milton's poetry. But what about unexplicit allusions in the prose? The Bohn edition with its notes by J.A. St. John had been available since 1848. One reference singled out by Bohn (3, 114–5 n.) that the *Index* does not pick up would seem obvious enough:

> in the Colleges so many of the young Divines, and those in next aptitude to Divinity have bin seene so oft upon the Stage writhing and unboning their Clergie limmes to all the antick and dishonest gestures of Trinculo's, Buffons, and Bawds; prostituting the shame of that ministry which either they had, or were nigh having, to the eyes of Courtiers and Court–Ladies, with their Groomes and *Madamoisellaes*. There while they acted, and overacted, among other young scholars, I was a spectator....
>
> (*Apology*, III, 300)

In *A Milton Dictionary* I duly indentified Trinculo as "a drunken sailor in *The Tempest*." Patterson in his 1933 *Student's Milton* Glossary (42) took the plural as generic: "clowns." There are problems. Can we believe that *The Tempest*, first printed in the First Folio of 1623, was, unprecedentedly, given a student performance at Cambridge at some time during Milton's residence there, 1625–32? It has been objected that *The Tempest* has no "Bawds."[18] The answer to that is: *bawd* in the seventeenth century could apply to a male (as well as female) procurer and Caliban counts as such when he promises Miranda to Stephano: "Aye, lord, she will become thy bed, I warrant" (III. 2. 112).

But there is a strong case––and an old one––for a clown of slightly later creation and similar name, Trincalo. In fact, Dr. Johnson, in quoting the *Apology* passage in his life of Milton, used the spelling "Trincalos." An appended note by Isaac Reed explains: "By the mention of this name, he evidently refers to Albumazar, acted at Cambridge, in 1614."[19] *Albumazar*, with its clown or buffoon Trincalo, a University play by Thomas Tomkis that was presented at the author's alma mater, Trinity College, March 9, 1615 (N.S.) before King James and Prince Charles–– and probably before Donne and George Herbert[20]––is a likelier candidate for revival in Milton's time. And, as Merritt Y. Hughes pointed out,[21] there is no problem in locating a bawd (female) among the characters.

Assuming that Milton did not himself suffer a misprint in 1642, Milton's Shakespearean spelling melds two drunks. What does the indexer, aware of this complication, do: put a question mark after Shakespeare and cross–reference Tomkis with another?

Will a 1985 adjunct to the Yale Milton (whose indexes are very eccentric) supersede the Patterson–Fogle *Index*? Awesome in bulk is the computer–begotten *Concordance to the English Prose of John Milton*, of which the general editors are Laurence Sterne and Harold H. Kollmeier and the publisher Medieval and Renaissance Texts and Studies, Binghamton. "[S]ome 44,000 lines of text had to be rendered into machine-readable format." This is the heftiest Milton reference book ever, slightly more than one foot tall and 9 1/4 inches wide and 3 1/4 inches thick. It weighs in at nine pounds, compared to seven for the two volumes of the *Index*. Would Harris Fletcher have found it a more pleasing object than he found the *Index*? "Two heavy volumes, each containing over a thousand pages on relatively thin paper are neither conducive to easy, frequent, and long continued use nor capable of withstanding it."[22] (If the paper had been thicker the volumes would have been heavier. Or would Fletcher have preferred *three* volumes?)

The 1491 pages of the *Concordance* contain a hundred thousand more entries than its predecessor, all lower case (vs. all initial capitals in Patterson-Fogle), and old spelling (vs. modernized). The old and variant spellings present many problems to a user who may never be wary enough, despite some general guidance in the preface. Did Milton ever use the word *indictment(s)*? You may need the *Index* to find out, for the *Concordance* has only *endightment*, *indighment*, and *inditements(s)*. Milton has *anough* much more often than *enough*, and *doe* more than *do*. Starting with *ambassadors* and *business*, the *Concordance* text has (by my count) forty-three *see also*'s: *see also* "embassadors"; *see also* "buisness." It could have done with more, or provided a cautionary list in the preface, commencing with the names *Aron* and *Austin*. *Phlegm*—will the user ever find his or her way to *fleam*? Running for *cover*, will you ever ground *coure*? Fortunately the *Oxford English Dictionary* is at hand to help.

The machine was fed a miswritten IBM card and therefore, in its brainlessness, spat out two ludicrous entries, *merce* and *nary*: because that was the way "mercenary" (correct in the Yale text) was presented. The result, of course, is that the occurrence of the word in *Church-Government* has gone unrecorded.

Covering less than half the body of Milton's works, but covering it totally (except for those common words normally omitted from concordances), Sterne-Kollmeier has obvious advantages and specialized uses (vocabulary study, frequency count), for those not exploring the Latin prose. (An early announcement made a promise that was not kept: "Useful frequency lists conclude the volume.") It keeps strictly to business (or "buisness"), no easily criticized branching out, no annotation, no judgment of what are the more important occurrences, little help on topics. You will get nowhere on the physical affliction by looking up "blindness," which is nearly always employed in the metaphorical sense. You will have no substitute for the fifty-six mostly pointed and poignant entries in the *Index*.

In sum, there is only one edition of the *opera omnia*, and, whatever its small percentage of flaws, we have a guide to the whole, generous and meticulous and Herculean. It may and does have rivals, but it has no substitute.[22]

NOTES

1.   (New York: Philosophical Library).
2.   My account amplifies but is indebted to John T. Shawcross's in William B. Hunter, Jr., general editor, *A Milton Encyclopedia* (Lewisburg: Bucknell University Press, 1978), 2, 71–2.
3.   David H. Stevens, *Reference Guide to Milton from 1800 to the Present Day* (Chicago: University of Chicago Press, 1930), 19, item 168.
4.   John Bradshaw in the preface to his own *Concordance*.
5.   Kerrigan, *The Sacred Complex: On the Psychogenesis of "Paradise Lost"* (Cambridge, Mass.: Harvard University Press, 1983), 244.
6.   These innocent followers of the Bohn reading (2, 68) include James Holly Hanford, Kathleen Hartwell, G. Wilson Knight, Sir Arthur Quiller-Couch, Sir Walter Raleigh, Denis Saurat, E.M.W. Tillyard, Basil Willey, besides some post-Bohn editions. See Le Comte, *Yet Once More: Verbal and Psychological Pattern in Milton* (New York: Liberal Arts Press, 1953), 149 (where the parallel 9, 224, is cited); *A Milton Dictionary*, s.v. "Bohn edition." The list could be rounded off with Cyrus R. Edmonds, *John Milton* (London: Cockshaw, 1851), 119, and Alden Sampson, *Studies in Milton* (New York, 1913), 72. The Revised Edition of Tillyard's *Milton* (New York: Collier, 1967), 134, has a corrective note (4): "`sees' is now the recognised reading." For the Yale *Pro Se Defensio* version, see Don M. Wolfe, ed., *Complete Prose Works of John Milton* (New Haven), 4 (1966), 795. *Yet Once More* (190, n. 19) points out that "The association of `see' and `seek' is as old as *Beowulf*, `seon and secean' (3102)."
7.   *ambones, antagony, apogaeum, apostemated, battology, bayard, bespaul, bezzling, billman, blains, breeze, brewess, budge, by-wipe, catena, cautelous, champerty, cog* (verb), *combust, commentitious, compellations, copesmate, coure, crambe, crasis, crudity, cullionly, dearn, debel, ding, dorrs, doss, dyscrasy, electuary, elenchs, enchiridion, ephod, ethnarch, euphrasy, evanges, exarchate, fadge, fescue(d), firelocks, frumps, fusil, gallipots, galloway, ging, gins, glebe, gleeking, glibbed, gripple, hacksters, haemony, halings, handsel, hecatontomes, hegemonicon, hip-shot, inducible, insulse-
-insulsity, jabberment, keal, keck, keel* (verb), *keri, kativ, legantine, legers, lesing, lin, loshes, loubel, lourdan, lozel, malestrand, malmsey, mammocks, manumise, maukin, mawls, megrim, meniaias* (not in the *OED*), *mincha, mostanend, nettlers, nomenclator, obtunding, omer, opiniaster, orcs, orts, oscitant, paragogical, pargetory, pargetted, peeling, pilchers, pismire, ponent, postil(ler)s,*

praxis, primero, prog, pudder, quiddities, quillets, quodlibets, redshanks, remora, runagates, sarcenet, scantling, scrannel, scrip, scrowl, sharked, shogging, sleekstone, slip–skin, slubbering snaffles, soldan, sord, sotadic, stales, subitanes, syntagma, teraphim, tetter, tine, tippet, tizzick, turms, ubiquitary, vagancies, villatic, whifflers, whippets, wincer, wind–eggs.

8.   See Milford C. Jochums, ed., *An Apology* (Urbana: University of Illinois Press, 1950), 21; Yale *Complete Prose*, 1 (1953), 878, 52.

9.   P.B. Tillyard, Milton's *Private Correspondence and Academic Exercises* (Cambridge: Cambridge University Press, 1932), 22; Yale *Complete Prose*, 2 (1959), 763; J. Max Patrick, general editor, Milton's *Prose* (New York: Doubleday, 1967), 613.

10. I am referring to Fletcher's 4–volume *Photographic Facsimile* edition of the *Complete Poetical Works* (Urbana: University of Illinois Press, 1943–8), in which the collation of the first edition of *PL*, for instance, was based on 146 copies, only to receive from Parker the devastating "Fletcher's *Milton*: A First Appraisal," *Papers of the Bibliographical Society of America*, 41 (1947), 33–52.

11. See Douglas Bush, ed., *A Variorum Commentary on the Latin and Greek Poems* (New York: Columbia University Press, 1970), 193–4.

12. *Autography* for "autograph," *Cruise* for "cruse," *Cythera* for "Cytherea," *Hortensisus* for "Hortensius" (s.v. *Citharess*), *nocturnal* for "nocturnal" (s.v. *Cotytto*). The conjectured reference to *Sanchuniathon* is not at "NS" but at IPA; for the first *Aonian* read line 17, not 18; for *Jonathans*, read V, not IV; for the first *Naiad*, read EL 7, not 6; for *Pylades*, read VIII, not VII; for Septimius *Severus*, the first reference should be X, not V.

13. Walter MacKellar, ed., *Paradise Regained* (New York: Columbia University Press, 1975), does cite Curtius for 2. 364 and 3. 31–4.

14. See the reprint of this *PMLA* article in Hanford, *John Milton, Poet and Humanist: Essays* (Cleveland: Press of Western Reserve University, 1966), 98, n. 147.

15. Patterson was following his own note in the back of *The Student's Milton*, 112. It happened that Alfred Stern had this view, *Milton und seine Zeit* (Leipzig: Von Duncker & Humblot, 1877), i, 2, 285–6. C.A. Patrides also goes for Comenius, *Selected Prose* (Penguin, 1974), 181; Hughes, for Hartlib, *Prose Selections* (New York: Odyssey Press, 1947), 29 (a note omitted from Hughes' widely used *Complete Poems and Major Prose* of 1957 [New York: Odyssey Press]). The (I think correct) vote for Hartlib goes back to Bohn, 3 (1848), 462, and forward to Charles Webster, ed., *Samuel Hartlib and the Advancement of Learning* (Cambridge:

Cambridge University Press, 1970), 2. "Reason is choice" but I have never encountered any reasoning on this matter.

16. Maurice Kelley and S.D. Atkins, "Milton and the Harvard Pindar," *Studies in Bibliography*, 17, 77–82.

17. On Milton–Shakespeare we now have Paul Stevens, *Imagination and the Presence of Shakespeare in "Paradise Lost"* (Madison: University of Wisconsin Press, 1985); on Milton–Spenser, besides the excellent entry by William B. Hunter, Jr. in *A Milton Encyclopedia*, 8 (1980), 34–6, the great proliferation of scholarship and criticism in the 1970's and 1980's is more or less covered by Gordon Teskey, "From Allegory to Dialectic: Imagining Error in Spenser and Milton," *PMLA*, 101 (1986), 9–23, to which should be added, Jonathan Goldberg, *Voice Terminal Echo: Postmodernism and English Renaissance Texts* (New Haven: Yale University Press, 1986).

18. Hugh G. Dick, ed., Thomas Tomkis, *Albumazar* (Berkeley: University of California Press, 1944), 54–5.

19. Samuel Johnson, *Works* (Oxford, 1825), 7, 70. Harris Fletcher compounds the confusion by spelling the *Albumazar* clown "Trinculo." *The Intellectual Development of John Milton*, 2 (Urbana: University of Illinois Press, 1961), 363. Some in quoting Johnson quoting Milton silently restore the Shakespearean name–– e.g., Edwin Paxton Hood, *John Milton: The Patriot and Poet* (London: Partridge & Oakey, 1852), 148.

20. For details see my "The Last Two Lines of Herbert's `The Forerunners,'" in *American Notes and Queries*, I, i (N.S.), 1988, 9–14.

21. Ed., Milton's *Complete Poems and Major Prose* (1957), 692, n. 21 (repeated from *Prose Selections*, 1947, 153).

22. Review in *Journal of English and Germanic Philology*, 40 (1941), 147.

23. For an example of ongoing use: "Simply to glance through Milton's overt allusions to Ovid, more than three hundred of which are noted in the Index to the Columbia *Works*, is to realize the pervasive nature of the relationship––no less, the difficulty of easily summarizing it." Richard J. DuRocher, *Milton and Ovid* (Ithaca, N.Y.: Cornell University Press, 1985) 36.

In the words of Roy Flannagan: "don't throw out your copy of the Index: it does put English poetry, Latin poetry, English prose, and Latin prose all together in one Big Picture. In no way are Sterne and Kollmeier trying to displace the work of Patterson and Fogle." *Milton Quarterly*, 20 (1986), 105.

MILTONIC ECHOES IN ELEGIA VII

William Hayley, Milton's biographer for the Romantics, has words of praise for the Seventh Elegy for showing "the youthful fancy of Milton under the influence of a sudden and vehement affection."[1] "Vehement" is a word that Milton in *Paradise Lost* (his prose uses are different) never employs without consciousness of its etymological meaning of *mindless*, as in "vehement desire" (8.526). The penultimate sentence of the Argument to Book 9 gives an aid to reading that some critics ignore at their own peril: "Adam, at first amazed, but perceiving her lost, resolves through the vehemence of love to perish with her." Nevertheless, taking it on its own terms, one could say that Elegia VII is a poem about disobedience to divine law, punishment, repentance, and supplication. (Compare the Argument to Book 10: "seek peace of the offended Deity by repentance and supplication.") It is one man's disobedience, but one line widens it out to mankind's ("genus humanum," 9). Suffering leads to faith, as the divinity says: "Et faciam vero per tua damna fidem" (30). God foresees that fallen Adam will be "Tried in sharp tribulation, and refined / By faith" (*PL* 11.63–64). The title of the future epic is anticipated, "amissum...caelum" (81) in a reference to the fall of the "proles Junonia" or Vulcan.[2] While Hughes designates Elegia VII "only a half–serious game with the traditional Ovidian theme of the poet's conquest by Cupid,"[3] he does not characterize the lines of retraction that follow hard upon it.[4] Are they also only half–serious, and if so, do two halves make a whole?

Whatever the tone, there is much in Milton's Latin that anticipates his more familiar English. The present writer's *Yet Once More: Verbal and Psychological Pattern in Milton* (17) gives one notable instance. It ultimately has to do with the poet's recurring fascination with the fate of Orpheus, with which he finds a parallel to his own potential or actual situation. In VII Orpheus does not surface (as against an abundance of other mythological lovers), but the fear of love (lightly presented) does. As Cupid predicts, "Nec te, stulte, tuae poterunt defendere Musae" (45).

119

This looks to two lines in "Lycidas": "What could the Muse herself that Orpheus bore, / The Muse herself, for her enchanting son" (58–59). A more literal translation is the lament for Orpheus in *Paradise Lost*: "Nor could the Muse defend / Her son" (7.37–38).

There is the case of the disappearing beloved. Bush freely translates "Ablata est, oculis non reditura meis" (76), "she...disappeared and left me dark, never again to return to my sight,"[5] thus pointing up connection with Adam's dream of Eve: "She disappeared, and left me dark" (8.478). Adam's dream had a happy realization. The verbally parallel dream of a deceased wife does not.[6] "Oculis non reditura meis" weirdly foretells the future: "thou / Revisit'st not these eyes" (3.22–23). Charles Diodati, soon to disappear forever, disappeared temporarily when Milton rushed to London to find him in September 1637; he was only "the shadow of a dream." Milton quoted the Greek words of Pindar (Pythian Odes, VIII, 95). (Columbia *Works*, 12. 20.)

The beauty preeminent in the crowd who smote the poet's heart and vanished—did it happen? Saurat, Tillyard, Fletcher, Broadbent, Parker were convinced it did, and Diekhoff inserted the poem in *Milton on Himself*.[7] The question is as out of fashion now as the one about whether Milton, at an early age, suffered from photophobia. As in the "Song: On May Morning" light brings May: "Now the bright morning star...leads with her / The flow'ry May" (1–3) (the editors fail to note "the flowrie Maye" in Giles Fletcher, *Christs Victorie in Heaven* (41.4); "Attulerat primam lux tibi, Maie, diem" ("Light had brought your first day, O May") (14). A hundred and forty years before Mutschmann speculated, Warton said of lines 15–16: "He really complains of the weakness of his eyes, which began early."[8] Landor was moved: "Here are two verses which I never have read without the heart-ache".[9] At any rate we have something that relates to other poems in, "At mihi adhuc refugam quaerebant lumina noctem, / Nec matutinum sustinuere jubar" ("But my eyes still sought the retreating night, and could not suffer the dazzling dawn"). Warton cited "light unsufferable" ("On the Morning of Christ's Nativity," 8). We cannot forget how Il Penseroso fled brightness, beginning with the explanation that Melancholy had to be shrouded because her "saintly visage" was "too bright / To hit the sense of human sight" (13–14)—shades (shall we say?) of "Dark with excessive bright thy skirts appear" (3.380)—and proceeding to the persona's avoidance of "Day's garish eye" "when the sun begins to fling / His flaring beams" (141, 131–32).

Girl-watching is better than sun-watching. L'Allegro also keeps an eye out for feminine beauty: "Where perhaps some beauty lies, / The cynosure of neighboring eyes" (79–80). It is not forbidden to look. How that theme reverberates through this author! Eve in *her* dream looks upon temptation, disturbed but sinless.

Fair it seemed,

Much fairer to my fancy than by day;
And as I wond'ring looked, beside it stood
One shaped and winged like one of those from heav'n
(5.52–55)

Not exactly Cupid. The moral position was proclaimed in *Areopagitica*: "I cannot praise a fugitive and cloister'd virtue...that never sallies out and sees her adversary" (Columbia *Works*, 4, 311). That stance, even to the first four letters of "fugitive," was enunciated in Elegia VII: "Haec ego non fugi spectacula grata severus" (57). Hughes, without noticing the parallel[10] (no editor does), aptly translates: "I did not turn puritanically away from the pleasant sights." The next two Latin lines--"Impetus et quo me fert juvenilis agor; / Lumina luminibus male providus obvia misi"--give an origin for "sallies" ("impetus") and the suggestion of an encounter that comes close to a battle, sending glances like darts. The rash inconsideration of consequences is emphasized in Bush's translation: "Instead I followed where youthful impulse led. With no thought beyond the moment, I sent my eyes to meet their eyes." Adam will not have this youthful bravado.

L'Allegro left the country for the city. The city or its suburbs was the dawnfall of the Milton of VII.

Towered cities please us then
And the busy hum of men,

....
With store of ladies, whose bright eyes
Rain influence   ("L'Allegro," 117ff.)

"Lumina luminibus." "Store of ladies" is the "turba frequens" of the corresponding Latin: "Et modo qua nostri spatiantur in urbe Quirites, / Et modo villarum proxima rura placent. / Turba frequens, facie simillima turba dearum, / Splendida per medias itque reditque vias" (51–54). William Cowper's rhymed version being too free, I essay my own:

In town where people take their ease,
Or where suburban meadows please,
A store of ladies, shining as gods,
Pass back and forth along the quads.

"Towered cities please us then"--this is the only "us" in "L'Allegro" and "Il Penseroso." Why does the poet switch from the personal pronoun singular? In VII we have the same phenomenon. After an unbroken series of singulars, such as "me" and "mihi" and "ego," the poet switches to the plural with line 62: "Principium nostri lux erat illa mali." With a poet so assured we are not going to say that he has "nostri" because "mei" would not fit metrically. I suggest that he is having intimations of *Paradise Lost*, and that the girl whose radiance or "lux" has smitten him is recognizably Eve's daughter. She has no name because her name is legion. In translating we may add an implied adjective: "That false light was the beginning of all our woe"--mankind's.[11]

Even Cupid, the conqueror of VII, is not too trivial to appear in *Paradise Lost*, provided he be called Love (which, after all, was also his name in the elegy--"Amor," 4, 17, 20). "Here Love his golden shafts employs, here lights / His constant lamp, and waves his purple wings" (4.763-64). Compare: "Astat Amor lecto, pictis Amor impiger alis; / Prodidit astantem mota pharetra deum" (17-18) and "Dixit, et, aurato quatiens mucrone sagittam" (47). ("Love stood beside my bed, hyperactive Love with the colored wings. His quiver, swaying, betrayed that it was the god standing there." "He spoke, shaking his gold-tipped shaft.")

Where did we last have "astat" beside a bed? "Ecce mihi subito praesul Wintonius astat" ("Lo and behold! all at once the Bishop of Winchester was standing there" Elegia III. 53). Why did the spirit of Lancelot Andrewes turn up at Milton's bed (as white and as obscurely seen as the "late espousèd saint" of thirty-two years later), and what does *he* have to do with Cupid? The answer to that question is, surprisingly much. The second half of Elegia III turns out to echo, with remarkable structural and verbal fidelity, Ovid's description of his amorous encounter with Corinna in *Amores* I.v.[12]

Thirty-eight years ago I recorded some half dozen repeated phrases between VII and Milton's other Latin poems.[13] I added that "he tried the trick `Fallor? an et' to begin lines in three different poems (El. V. 5; El. VII. 56; `In Prodit. Bomb.,' 3) before he carried it over into English in *Comus*, `Was I deceived, or' (221)" (*Yet Once More*, 105). Of greater interest is line 100 at the end: "Nescio cur, miser est suaviter omnis amans" ("Not for me to say why, but every lover is sweetly miserable"). This oxymoron links with Philomel "In her sweetest, saddest plight" ("Il Penseroso," 57). I once asked but now add a passage in support: "Does `sweetest, saddest' give the ambivalence of forbidden pleasure? Ostensibly `sweetest' refers to music-making power, `saddest' to the circumstances whereby Philomela became a nightingale."[14] If Milton and Philomela suffered in their very different ways from carnal passion, so did Satan confronting "the dear pledge / Of Dalliance" with Sin and speaking to her of "joys / Then sweet, now sad to mention" (2.819-20). True, the simultaneity is not there. Nothing is sweet now except in memory. Rhetorically, although not verbally (as we watch Milton transferring his *ars poetica* from Latin verse to English), it would be purer to cite the "sweet poison" oxymoron in *Comus*. That sweet poison was "the sweet poison of misusèd wine" (47), but other writers of the Renaissance, including Mantuan, applied the expression to love (*venenum* as deriving from *Venus*).[15] Angelo Poliziano, addressing Love, said, "Nudrusci l'alme d'un dolce veneno" ("You fill souls with a sweet poison") (*Stanze per La Giostra*, Book I, line 12). The paradox even turns up in a mid–nineteenth–century German romance about Milton, which has him drawn to Alice Egerton: "As Abélard and Héloise in times of yore drew the sweet poison of love from the cup of science and investigation, so here, too, the growing affection stole under the mask of thirst [*Comus*!] for learning and intellectual improvement into the hearts of Milton and Alice."[16]

Leaving these byways, let us conclude by stretching forward to Milton's last poems. Line 90 reads (continuing the latter half's pattern of plural pronouns): "Forte nec ad nostras surdeat illa preces" ("Perhaps she would not be deaf to our prayers"). The sexes are reversed in *Samson Agonistes* when Dalila complains, "I see thou art implacable, more deaf / To prayers than winds and seas" (960–61). Milton has left far behind the convention that it is the man who begs. It was the girl who was "made of hard adamant" ("duro...est adamante creata," 89) or Milton who needed to be ("d'intero diamante," Son. VI. 8: the *Variorum* on this cites Columbia *Works* III, 313–14, "arming in compleat diamond"). Finally it is Jesus: "Proof against all temptation as a rock / Of adamant, and as a center firm" ("firm" translates "duro") (*Paradise Regained* 4.533–34). Womankind is "scorned" in three languages, and laughed at in two. "Atque tuum sprevi maxime 'numen, Amor" (4) is etymon, as regards the verb and one noun, to "io, ch' Amor spreggia soléa" (Son. IV. 2): "Easily I scorned your divinity, Love": "I who was wont to scorn Love." This prepares for a history lesson (forty years later) from Satan to Belial: "How many have with a smile made small account / Of beauty and her lures, easily scorned / All her assaults?" (*Paradise Regained* 2.193–95). What was the origin of that smile and those lures? Line 3 of Sonnet IV: "Quel ritroso io, ch' Amor spreggiar soléa / E de' suoi lacci spesso mi ridéa" ("That cantankerous I, who was wont to scorn Love, and often laughed at his snares"). "Spesso" is the "Saepe" of the preceding line of the Elegy, "assaults" the "sagittas" of the same line. The words even have obvious affinities of sound. "Echo, sweetest nymph that liv'st unseen" (*Comus*, 230), a "thousand echoes" (Nativity Hymn, 100)--she, they, may be elusive but are not beyond capturing.

There is a problem in the Latin with "surdeat" (90). Carey commented: "An incorrect form; there is no verb *surdeo*."[17] This is true for those who have the advantage of modern dictionaries, such as *Harpers' Latin Dictionary* or, now, the *Oxford Latin Dictionary*. There is no classical instance of *surdeo*. But Robertus Stephanus, *Thesaurus Linguae Latinae*, has an entry for *surdeo*, citing an epigram by the German humanist Euricius Cordus. St. Paul's School would have had the dictionaries of Sir Thomas Elyot–Thomas Cooper, Thomasius, and Rider–Holyoke, all of which admit the word that Carey says does not exist. Milton can hardly be blamed for relying on the dictionaries available to him. Had he felt vulnerable to the posthumously published sneer of Salmasius, *Ad Johannem Miltonum Responsio*[18]--as he did in regard to a couple of quantities, which he changed--he could readily have altered the line to, "Forte nec ad nostras surda eat illa preces" ("Perhaps she would not go away deaf to our prayers").

Milton's progress is from the light, playful, even trivial, very possibly wholly imaginary, to the most serious and believable. (Fictitious suffering is replaced by real. In the elegy Apollo's serpent is beneficent; we cannot care that Amphiaraus went to Orcus; we do not picture the conclusion: Milton spitted on a cupidean shaft with his girl.) Artifice is the apprentice to art. The beauty who, even if she did not exist, could be an object of longing, is wished to be seen. "O utinam spectare semel mihi detur amatos / Vultus" ("O would that it might be given me yet once more to see the loved features") (87). The husband of the "late espousèd saint"--that second marriage,[19] at least, was made in heaven--has theologically justified hope: "And such as yet once more I trust to have / Full sight of her in heaven without restraint" (Son. XIX. 7-8).

Yet once more, Milton in Elegia VII "makes evident," as B. Rajan has phrased it, "the unifying energy of the creative mind at work and the persistence over many years of that mind's basic patterns."[20] In particular there is the "paradise lost" theme. Milton was early seized with the Freudian insight that the only paradises are those we have lost. We come back to line 76 as central, "Ablata est, oculis non reditura meis": "She was taken away, never again to return to my sight." "But O as to embrace me she inclined, / I waked, she fled, and day brought back my night" (Son. XIX. 13-14). We do not know that John Milton sorely missed his lost childhood; we are doubtful that he had one to miss. But lost women and lost friends (not to say lost utopias)--they haunt his life and work: Lycidas, Damon, Mary Powell Milton (twice lost), Katherine Woodcock Milton, Eve, Proserpine. They cost him pain to seek them through his poetry. They passed out of sight. No wonder that, in compensation, *Paradise Lost* has its "many representations of intrusive and aggressive seeing."[21] With such resonance, the lost she in Elegia VII, if she did not exist, had to be invented.

NOTES

1. Hayley, *The Life of Milton* (1796), 21.
2. Both phrases were utilized twice. As noted in Edward Le Comte, *Yet Once More: Verbal and Psychological Pattern in Milton* (New York: Liberal Arts Press, 1953), 105, "proles Junonia" occurs in a line of "Naturam non pati Senium" (23) that anticipates *Paradise Lost*. 1.746. Douglas Bush, ed., *A Variorum Commentary on the Latin and Greek Poems* (New York: Columbia University Press, 1970), 139, notes "amissi coeli solatium" in Prolusio V, Columbia *Works*, 12, 190.
3. Merritt Y. Hughes, ed., Milton's *Complete Poems and Major Prose* (New York: Odyssey Press, 1957), 58. This widely used edition does not translate line 8 or "melius" in line 43.
4. Separated by a rule in 1645 and 1673. Thomas Newton's editions substituted a space for the rule and, misleadingly, continued the line numbering begun with VII. William Cowper's rhymed version treated the two poems as one.
5. Bush, *The Complete Poetical Works* (Boston: Houghton Mifflin, 1965), 47. I follow this text for the Latin and English poems. Unattributed translations are mine.
6. Le Comte, 15–17.
7. Denis Saurat, *Milton: Man and Thinker* (New York: Dial Press, 1925), 7; E.M.W. Tillyard, *Milton*, rev. ed. (London: Collier, 1966), 22; Harris F. Fletcher, ed., *Complete Poetical Works* (Boston: Houghton Mifflin, 1941), 505; J.B. Broadbent, *Some Graver Subject* (London: Schocken Books, 1967), 31; William R. Parker, *Milton: A Biography* (Oxford: Oxford University Press, 1968), 1, 77; John S. Diekhoff (New York: Oxford University Press, 1939), 31. Twenty years later Fletcher was more ambiguous: "*Elegia VII* is a revelation of a personal experience, probably much more the work of Milton's imagination than real" (*The Intellectual Development of John Milton*, 2 [Urbana, Ill.: University of Illinois Press, 1961], 415).
8. Thomas Warton, ed., *Poems* (1785), 480. Heinrich Mutschmann quotes this in *The Secret of John Milton* (Dorpat, 1925), 3.
9. Walter Savage Landor, *Imaginary Conversations*, "Southey and Landor," Second Conversation, *Works* (London: Edward Moxon, 1846), 2, 171.
10. First printed in Le Comte, *Milton's Unchanging Mind* (Port Washington, N.Y.: Kennikat Press, 1973), 96, n. 69.
11. After submitting my manuscript I discovered I have been anticipated (and reinforced) on this point by Robert Hodge, editor

with John Broadbent, *Samson Agonistes, Sonnets, etc.* (Cambridge: Cambridge University Press, 1977), 76–77: "The line has an ominous generality, later to be echoed in *PL* I.1." Anthony Low comments: "the style and subject matter of the Cupid passages resemble epic delineation of single combat." "*Elegia Septima*: The Poet and the Poem," *Milton Studies*, 19 (1984), 27.

12.   As detailed in "Sly Milton: The Meaning Lurking in the Contexts of His Quotations."

13.   Le Comte, *Yet Once More*, 160, n. 45: "Twice to begin a line with `tu modo da' (El. IV, 61; El. VII, 101) is scarcely to arouse comment, and the same is true of two other desiderative formulae, `O utinam' (El. I, 21; El. VII, 87) and `Parce precor' (El. VII, 93; Prodit. Bomb. II, 4). `Crede mihi' begins five lines (El. V, 91; El. VI, 6, 43; El. VII, 91; In Prodit. Bomb. II, 10),...`Nec mora' three (El. III, 35; El. VII, 69; In Q.N., 208), `Ast ego' three (El. I, 85; El. IV, 57; El. VII, 77)."

14.   *Yet Once More*, 63. Robert Browning's *Balaustion's Adventure* commences with the line (later repeated), "About that strangest, saddest, sweetest song" (a reference to Euripides' *Alcestis*). Cf. "Dulcis amaror," El. I, 40.

15.   Mantuan's "Faustus. Aegloga prima": "Hoc animi tam triste bonum tam dulce uenenum," 119 (in Fred J. Nichols, *An Anthology of Neo-Latin Poetry* [New Haven: Yale University Press, 1979]). I am adding to the catalogue of references given in Le Comte, *Poets' Riddles: Essays in Seventeenth-Century Explication* (Port Washington, N.Y.: Kennikat Press, 1975), 97, n. 84. Bono Giamboni gets us back to *Comus* by quoting St. Augustine: "L'ebrietà è lusinghiere demonio, dolce veleno, soave peccato" (*Giardano di consolazione* [Florence, 1856], 173).

16.   Max Ring, *John Milton and His Times: An Historical Novel*, trans. F. Jordan (New York: Appleton: 1868), 48. This is faithful to the original German: "das süsse Gift der Liebe," 78 of *John Milton und seine Zeit* (Frankfurt a. Main, 1857). On Ring see Elizabeth K. Hill, "Ring about Milton: A German Novelist's View," *Milton Quarterly*, 16 (1982), 97–98.

17.   John Carey, ed. with Alastair Fowler, *The Poems* (London: Longmans, 1968), 73.

18.   See John B. Dillon, "*Surdeo*, Saumaise, and the Lexica: An Aspect of Milton's Latin Diction," *Humanistica Lovaniensia*, 27 (1978), 238–52.

19.   It is evident that I am with the majority against two heresies: one, that Mary Powell Milton is the subject of the sonnet; two, that *Samson Agonistes* is not Milton's last poem. I began marshalling points against the former in "The Veiled Face of Milton's Wife," *Notes & Queries*, n.s., I (1954), 245–46, and continued in *A Milton*

Dictionary (New York: Philosophical Library, 1961), 311–12. I argued against the latter in "New Objections to a Pre–Restoration Date for *Samson Agonistes*," *Poets' Riddles*, 129–60.

20. Rajan, ed., *The Prison and the Pinnacle* (Toronto: University of Toronto Press, 1973), 110. In 1823 Leigh Hunt remarked "how completely the Latin Milton answers to the English: how suitab.e the conceptions of the young Latin poet are to those of the author of `Lycidas' and `Penseroso,' and consequently of the future author of the *Paradise Lost*"; Joseph A. Wittreich, Jr., ed., *The Romantics on Milton* (Cleveland: Case Western Reserve University Press, 1970), 418–19. The pattern of Milton's borrowing from himself is made more intricate when he is also borrowing from someone else. To give a new instance in this area, the inscription to Patrick Young (Columbia *Works* 18, 269) ends, "paucis h[u]jusmodi lectorib[us] contentus," which is Horace's "Contentus paucis lectoribus" (*Sat.* I. 10. 74). We move forward from 1645 to *Paradise Lost* and the famous "fit audience find, though few" (7.31). Newton's statement, "He had Horace in mind," is strengthened by Milton's earlier quotation. (For five other examples of this theme in Milton see *Yet Once More*, 121–22.)

21. William Kerrigan, *The Sacred Complex: On the Psychogenesis of "Paradise Lost"* (Cambridge: Harvard University Press, 1983), 244.

JUSTA EDOVARDO KING

The story, though not the book, is familiar and has been outlined in a thousand introductions: how Edward King, born in Ireland but of a distinguished English family (his father Sir John was Privy Councillor for Ireland and Secretary to the Irish Government), entered Christ's College, Cambridge, June 9, 1626 at age fourteen some sixteen months after Milton, after tuition by Thomas Farnaby, the famous schoolmaster; how King, three years younger than Milton and academically junior by one year, received by royal mandate, June 10, 1630, just after his B.A., a fellowship such as Milton never received; how, besides being Tutor and Fellow in Christ's, King served as prelector, 1634–5, while qualifying for the church; how he planned during the Long Vacation of 1637 to visit his friends and relatives in Dublin, including his and Milton's first tutor, William Chappell (with whom Milton as a freshman had had a quarrel that resulted in Milton's rustication), who was serving there as Provost of Trinity College; how King thoughtfully made his will nine days before setting sail from Chester; how the ship, while still not far from the Welsh coast, struck a rock and went down, King last being seen on his knees in prayer; how a memorial volume was planned and Milton at Horton was invited to contribute, his pastoral monody "Lycidas" occupying the last pages of a small quarto[1] of thirty–six poems, thirteen in English, twenty in Latin, three in Greek.

Ben Jonson, who was buried in Westminster Abbey August 9, 1637, the day before Edward King was drowned, was to be honored by Oxford University with *Jonsonus Virbius: or The Memory of Ben Jonson, Revived by the Friends of the Muses.* This volume was, like the *Justa*, published early in 1638 in a sort of friendly rivalry between the sister universities. One poet, John Cleveland, contributed to both collections. Cleveland, like Milton, had no connection with Oxford. The latter as Jonson's greatest heir as a classical––or even courtly––poet should have been asked to contribute to *Jonsonus Virbius*, but he had chosen to hide the light of his genius under a bushel––the initials J.M. for "Lycidas," not

129

even initials for the lines on Shakespeare in the 1632 Folio (his first publication), anonymity likewise for the *Maske*, which was published by Henry Lawes in 1637 with a shrinking-violet motto from Virgil,[2] other early masterwork just lying around in manuscript.

Michael Honywood's second Latin poem bravely wished that Edward might be Virbius, and everybody remembers Milton's praise of King as poet (was King the surrogate in his mind for Jonson?), but of course there could be no comparison of abilities with the late poet laureate. The twenty-five-year-old Cambridge graduate is not known to have written in English. Appropriately, the Jonson memorial volume is predominantly in English, in contrast to the hexameters, elegiacs, Alcaics and Greek choriambiacs brought out for King. King's surviving Latin ventures into verse, most of them obstetric pieces on royal births, showed little promise that he would ever "build the lofty rhyme," but that was not the point. To the point were, to judge by the repeated references, his virtue, his piety, his learning, his promise, and his connections.

Parker traced thirty-three surviving copies of the 1638 *Justa*.[3] Izaak Walton owned a copy.[4] Several copies have corrections of "Lycidas" in a hand resembling Milton's.[5] There have been two reprints. One was brought out in Dublin (in modern typeface) in 1835 by William J. Thornhill of Trinity College (R. Graisberry was the University printer). It had no apparatus of any sort. In 1939 Columbia University Press published for the Facsimile Text Society a reproduction of the original edition, with an introduction by Ernest C. Mossner. This has been long out of print. The present edition offers the first translations, plus such notes as seemed most urgent.

The book is so little known that scholars do not even count the number of poems in it right. One speaks of "33 poems,"[6] two others of "nineteen Latin"[7]. A fourth declares Milton "wrote much the longest poem in the *Justa*,"[8]--which is what Felton did. A well-known editor got mixed up on Milton's title.[9] The few discussions there have been have pretty much walked the narrow round of the English poems, giving such notices a distorting imbalance. "Lycidas" is not to be defined or understood only by its "native language." It is Virgil, for instance, who provides the basis for such strange expressions as "But now my oat proceeds," and "Phoebus...touch'd my trembling eares," and "meditate the...Muse." We had better gain access to what Milton read, no matter what the language, and he certainly read the *Justa*, may, indeed--it has been conjectured[10]-- have seen the other poems before, around November 1637, he wrote his.

It is a fact of our time that American Ph.D.'s do critical and research articles on "Lycidas" in total ignorance of Latin and Greek and have ignored the first twenty-three poems that accompanied it because they could not read them. Sorry indications of the prevailing cultural situation abound. Miltonists with some Latin can be found mistranslating (*absit omen*); others with no Latin do not even bother to check tags before rushing into print: a famous book of 1954 has "sub specie eternitas"; an article that ends in total confusion begins with "in media res." A 1990 blurb announces a new poem with the same new Latin: "In keeping with classic epic formula, `Canto One: In Media Res' opens--" no, not quite. A collaboration will give us the typical present-day split: an article on a neo-Latin source of *Comus* that commissioned a translation; an anthology of pastoral elegy edited by one person and translated by another; an edition of George Sandys' version of Ovid's *Metamorphoses* (1632) that had to be entrusted to two professors of classics, since a professor of English capable of handling it (such as Douglas Bush, who wrote the introduction) is now *rara avis in terris*. Exemplifying the spirit of the times is a piece in the *Publications* of the Modern Language Association (which no longer publishes articles in foreign languages, even elementary French cannot be quoted without translation) that was issued in 1976 to much fanfare. The editor praised it vociferously. The author chimed in with regrets that he could not spend even more time acquiring "new bits of information." Meanwhile one bit of information that he did print was that "VIXI" means "I have conquered." A whole superstructure of faddish numerology is built upon this. The author in turn was following without question a previous author. His gaffe passed at least two consultants, six members of the editorial board of *PMLA*, and the editor-in-chief. Moreover, even after attention was called, this group, indifferent to mere detail, awarded the article the William Riley Parker Prize as the "outstanding" article of the year. Egregious it is. It is a heavy irony that the name of the late Professor Parker, that meticulous scholar (whose first book was on a classical subject), should be used to honor a would-be exegete who neither knows nor bothers to check a common Latin word. As a colleague, not caring whether he sounded male-chauvinist, remarked to me, "Even my wife knows `Veni, vidi, vici.'" So did Rosalind (*As You Like It* V. ii. 34). An otherwise excellent 1979 book pricks itself on "paradisial petals *sine spinae*."

I do not maintain esthetic deprivation has resulted from ignorance of the *Justa*. The opening poem (which essays the senarius) spoke all too truly of the danger that King would be done in again by bad verse. Hilaire Belloc[11] (who knew how to write verse) singled out two couplets as hard to forget: "The early Mattens which you daily said, / And Vespers, when you dwelt next doore Saint Chad" (16); and, "Whiles Phebus shines within our Hemisphere, / There are no starres, or at least none appear" (8). Ogden Nash might have boggled at the rhyme (11) of "diviner, and" with "not Ireland." Milton's poem, besides being the only pastoral, is the only poem of quality. Genius apart, he has the decorum and control that come with maturity: it is to be remarked that most of the contributors were five to fourteen years his junior. Potts, who wrote in Greek, was a boy of fifteen, King's sizar. Most are schoolboys in artistry, aiming for the sublime and hitting the ridiculous. Dr. Johnson could not tolerate the mixture in "Lycidas" of sacred and profane, "irreverend [sic] combinations" that "approach to impiety,"[12] but true temerity comes with W. More's likening of King's behavior in the storm to Jesus': a seventeenth-century reader crossed out the offending lines and wrote "Blasphemy" in the margin.[13] The reader, no matter what his background, will soon weary of puns on *King*, complaints to the marine deities and muses, conceits on salt seas and salt tears and on sunken treasure, trite mythological allusions, words chosen either for metrical convenience or rhyme. One of the rarer words, *Phoebicolae* (1 and 6), Milton himself had used at age seventeen in Elegia I (line 14). Joseph Scaliger had set his seal on the usage[14] (nothing in these exercises is done without permission), even as his father Julius Caesar Scaliger laid it down that an epicedium had five parts: Praise, Narration, Lamentation, Consolation, Exhortation.[15] The grammatical and lexical correctness of these youths seems unassailable, at least to a casual and relatively untrained modern onlooker. The three Greek poems, short though they are, take longer and surer flight in that language than Milton ever did. I could not help but be impressed by William Iveson's studied avoidance of Attic in favor of Aeolic, Epic, and Doric. Candidly, it took much thumbing of the reference grammars to discover that that form of the genitive in the first line had precedent. But these academic versifiers always have precedent. So did "Lycidas," which they often sound as if they were parodying. Theirs is a case not of "The Survival of the Pagan Gods"--to quote Jean Seznec's title--but of a rat-tat-tat on very dry bones.

    One may learn something about both King and "Lycidas" from them. About King: R. Brown (and only he) gives the information that King was blond. This is part of a conventional comparison to Phoebus, but "flavo" is an inconceivable description (in this circle of intimates) if King's hair was, for instance, black. And a light complexion makes more feasible the several sun comparisons. The immediately following poem by J.B. indicates that King kept a commonplace book (like Milton). There is so much emphasis on the young man's learning--the "learned Friend" of Milton's 1645 headnote--that we seem to be going beyond convention to fact. King was, after all, already an experienced teacher, perhaps escaped envy by precociously deserving the fellowship he got by fiat, had a book with him when he went down (as did Shelley), gives the impression of a cloistered scholar with a pedantic scorn for the vernacular. When he praised a contemporary play it was an academic Latin comedy, and he lauded it for its decency.[16] He is twice likened to Scaliger. His will mentions, first of all, his books. In R. Mason's poem he gives encouragement to the fledgling poet, like Milton's "old Dametas."

    The "fatall and perfidious bark" of "Lycidas," 100 echoes Hall's "fatall bark" and Coke's "Infida pinus, navis inhospita."[17] "Qua Deva tribuit maris potenti / Vectigalis aquas Deo" (11) parallels "where Deva spreads her wisard stream." In several of the elegies King is a sun that set:

he rises only on pages 8, 13, and 25 of the English section. Dolphins and nymphs and flowers are dispersed throughout. "Ah me, I fondly dream!"––Nicholas Felton strikes this plaintive note in Latin. Milton's reference to King's unmarried state, to be rewarded by "unexpressive nuptial song" in heaven, is almost unique, but not quite: the first poem in the book has one Greek word, applied to Thetis the sea, that means "virgin–killing." Reference to male virginity, like the later reference to Diodati's in "Epitaphium Damonis," may cause snickers in the modern classroom; a professor is glad to be able to show it is not entirely peculiar. Similarly, Milton was out of step with our time when in *Areopagitica* he started his famous assertion that "a good book is the precious lifeblood of a master spirit" with "Many a man lives a burden to the earth." The New York Public Library carries only the latter part of the sentence over the entrance to its reading room; the first part would look like an attack on welfare. But Milton meant that discrimination, or rather death's lack of discrimination, for he had said the same long before in Elegia II, in mourning the university beadle: why does not death, he asked, carry off, instead, the numerous tribe "qui pondus inutile terrae" (19)? The sentiment of a haughty and callous aristocrat, elitist, snob? Comparatively not, when we align it with the view of the privileged younger brother of Edward King that mass deaths of ordinary people, such as occur in wars or plagues or famine, refresh the land and only make cities look brighter, the dregs removed.

That effete snob was Henry King, who sang in both sections and may have been the prime instigator of the volume. He is not to be confused with Henry King the future bishop of Chichester,[18] author of "The Exequy," who contributed to *Jonsonus Virbius*. The latter's great and famous lines on his deceased wife are followed at some distance by the tribute in *Justa* of a brother to a brother:

> But heark! My pulse like a soft Drum
> Beats my approch, tells Thee I come;
> And slow howere my marches be,
> I shall at last sit down by Thee.

> Meanwhile let me poore, senselesse,
> dead, alone
> Sit and expect my resurrection,
> To follow him; two sorrows sure will do,
> That he is dead, that I am not dead too. (2)

Was there some literary interaction between Milton and Thomas Norton, 1615–91, fellow of Christ's? Had Norton seen, and, like numerous readers since, had doubts about a sun–in–bed conceit in the Ode "On the Morning of Christ's Nativity" that had been written nine years before out would not be published until 1645? "So when the sun in bed, / Curtained with cloudy red, / Pillows his chin upon an orient wave." (stanza xxvi) This is the *rising* sun; quaintness is mitigated by connection made with the Son of God. The poet therefore does not have Apollo, who is better entitled to a chin and a pillow. Norton (19) reproaches all such conceits: "Poets, then leave your wonted strain; [a pun!] / For now you may no longer feigne / Apollo, when he goes to bed, / O'th' western billows [an echo of *pillows*?] layes his head: / I'th Irish sea, there set our Sun; / And since he's set, the day's undone." Of course the author of "Lycidas" would outdo both Norton and himself with,

> Weep no more, wofull shepherds, weep no more;
> For Lycidas your sorrow is not dead,
> Sunk through he be beneath the watry floore:
> So sinks the day--starre in the Ocean bed,
> And yet anon repairs his drooping head,
> And tricks his beams, and with new spangled ore
> Flames in the forehead of the morning sky:
> So Lycidas sunk low, but mounted high...(24–5)

As mentioned, there is no shortage of puns on the subject's name. The first poem has (A 3v) "Kingus obiit; Rex artium"--then runs through Princeps, Imperator, Tyrannus, Monarcha, and Caesar. Canon John Hayward (29) makes King a sort of star-kissed tuna: "He is King of the ocean, whom the ocean covers. If it is asked what the price is for being king of the sea, know that for this title you lose your life." Recent conjectures have Milton joining this wordplay. Did the future Lycidas take the part of Substance in the festivities commemorated in "At a Vacation Exercise": "O'er all his brethren he shall reign as King" (75)? (The Rivers are interjected because Relation was played by a son of Sir John Rivers-- a ten-line joke.)[19] "Genius of the shore," "Lycidas," 183: the transformation into a tutelary deity or lighthouse recalls the etymology of "Edward," given by Camden as "happy keeper."[20] The commentators have neglected the Apocrypha to their loss: "And in the day of the king's birth every month they were brought by bitter constraint to eat of the sacrifices; and when the feast of Bacchus was kept, the Jews were compelled to go in procession to Bacchus, carrying ivy." 2 Maccabees 6. 7. E.E. Duncan-Jones' letter to the *Times Literary Supplement* (Aug. 24–30, 1990, 895) observes: "The line of *Lycidas* that combines the words `bitter constraint,' it will be remembered, rhymes at a little distance with `ivy never sere': and the poet's dealings with ivy are like those of the Jews, reluctant. Whether `the day of the king's birth' linked itself in Milton's mind with the day of King's death must be uncertain."

Three of the contributors to *Justa*, Joseph Beaumont and Cleveland and Henry More, went on to fame, or notoriety, as poets. "R.C." may or may not be Richard Crashaw (his verses have been mistranslated in a 1970 edition). The *Dictionary of National Biography* details the eminence of five others: Farnaby, Honywood, Charles Mason, Pearson, Widdrington. William Hall, a student at Christ's College from 1628 to 1635, did twenty-two lines on Hobson that are at the Folger library.[21] Other names appear in John Peile's *A Biographical Register of Christ's College.*[22]

What does the dedication to "P.M.S." mean? Some rather desperate conjectures, including one of my own, should be abandoned in favor of the once standard "Piis manibus sacrum" ("Consecrated to his pious shade").[23] This leaves us without any alphabetical clue as to who perpetrated that clumsy (David Masson's word) run-on sentence.

In all this leaden mediocrity, all the worse for being fancy, the only initials that count are those on the last page, "J.M."

NOTES

1. Not "small octavo," as Sir Charles Oman plausibly states on the first page of a spirited article riddled with inaccuracies (his first sentence says that "Lycidas" has "200 and odd lines"), "Of Poor Mr. King, John Milton, and Certain Friends," *Cornhill Magazine*, 156 (1937), 577–87.

2. See, further, "Sly Milton: The Meaning Lurking in the Contexts of his Quotations," above, 102–3.

3. W.R. Parker, *Milton: A Biography* (Oxford: Oxford University Press, 1968), 2, 814; Parker and David A. Randall, *An Exhibit of Seventeenth–Century Editions of Writings by John Milton* (Bloomington, 1969), item 4.

4. Parker, 2, 814; J. Milton French, *Life Records of John Milton* (1949; rpt. New York: Gordian, 1966), 1, 356.

5. French, 1, 355; cf. 5, 384.

6. Watson Kirkconnell, *Awake the Courteous Echo: The Themes and Prosody of "Comus," "Lycidas," and "Paradise Regained" in World Literature with Translations of Major Analogues* (Toronto: University of Toronto Press, 1973), 243.

7. Mossner, Introduction to *Justa Edovardo King*, vii; J.B. Leishman, *Milton's Minor Poems* (Pittsburgh: University of Pittsburgh Press, 1969), 247. This mysterious miscount goes back through the nineteenth century to the eighteenth: Thomas Keightley, *An Account of the Life, Opinions, and Writings of John Milton* (London: Chapman & Hall, 1855), 289; Thomas Warton (who is repeated in Henry John Todd's nineteenth–century editions), ed., Milton's *Poems Upon Several Occasions* (London, 1791), 37; Francis Peck, *New Memoirs of the Life and Poetical Works of Mr. John Milton* (London, 1740), 35.

8. David H. Stevens, *Milton Papers* (Chicago: University of Chicago Press, 1927), "The Will of Edward King," 37.

9. The first printing of Merritt Hughes' edition of *Complete Poems and Major Prose* (New York: Odyssey Press, 1957), began the discussion of "Lycidas," 116, with: "The title *Lycidas* was first given to this poem in Milton's edition of his *Poems...both English and Latin* in 1645. It had previously been published simply as `A Monody' at the end of a collection of elegies, the *Obsequies of Edward King*," etc. A.W. Verity, ed., *"Ode on the Morning of Christ's Nativity," "L'Allegro," "Il Penseroso" and "Lycidas"* (Cambridge: Pitt Press, 1891), xxxix, note 1, cited two others as making this mistake.

10. Michael Lloyd, *"Justa Edouardo King,"* NQ, 5 (1958), 432–4; Leishman, 249 ff. There have been conjectures with a less specific basis, such as William P. Trent's "Is it possible that the poems were submitted to Milton for revision and arrangement..?" Ed., *"L'Allegro," "Il Penseroso," "Comus,"* and *"Lycidas"* (New York: Longmans, 1897), 61, n. 1. I should answer No: the poems have not been revised.

11. *Milton* (Philadelphia: Lippincott, 1935), 119–20.

12. "Life of Milton" in *Works* (Oxford, 1825), 7, 120.

13. Parker–Randall, *An Exhibit,* item 4.

14. Douglas Bush, ed., *Variorum Commentary on The Latin and Greek Poems* (New York: Columbia University Press, 1970), 1, 49.

15. *Poetics,* excerpted in Scott Elledge, ed., *Milton's "Lycidas"* (New York: Harper & Row, 1966), 109.

16. See King's Latin iambics prefixed to Peter Hausted's *Senile Odium* as quoted by Warton (and repeated in Todd's editions), 39.

17. Noted by Leishman, 252.

18. Two excellent editors who fall into this mistaken identity trap are Verity, xxxvii, n. 1, and John B. Broadbent, ed., Milton's *Odes, Pastorals, Masques* (Cambridge: Cambridge University Press, 1975), 222–3; as well as Lois Potter, *A Preface to Milton* (New York, Scribner, 1971), 83. Verity on p. xli next identifies Henry King as Edward's brother: did he think the brother became bishop of Chichester? Broadbent is innovative in gathering together the literature of drowning and for a quotation from Mircea Eliade's *Shamanism* (London, 1964) that throws a sweeping light on "Lycidas" *and* the *Justa*: "In water everything is `dissolved', every `form' is broken up, everything that has happened ceases to exist...Immersion is the equivalent, at the human level, of death at the cosmic level, of the cataclysm (the Flood) which periodically dissolves the world into the primeval ocean. Breaking up all forms, doing away with the past, water possesses this power of purifying, or regenerating, of giving new birth...Water purifies and regenerates because it nullifies the past, and restores—even if only for a moment—the integrity of the dawn of things" (Broadbent, 187).

19. For references see Le Comte, *A Dictionary of Puns in Milton's English Poetry* (New York: Columbia University Press, 1981), *s.vv.*

20. J. Karl Franson, "Etymology of Edward King's Name," *Milton Quarterly*, 22 (1988), 127–28.

21. 2, 765, item 9. Parker nowhere mentions that Hall contributed to *Justa*.

22. Gordon Campbell, *Milton Quarterly*, 17 (1983), 59.

23. Le Comte, quoting private communication from G.W. Pigman III, *MQ*, 16 (1982), 83; Jeremy Maule, *MQ*, 18 (1984), 135–36.

Franson has ingeniously reckoned that "the only highly probable site for the disaster" to "that fatal and perfidious bark" ("Lycidas," 100) was Coal Rock off the northern coast of Anglesey. "The Fatal Voyage of Edward King, Milton's Lycidas," *Milton Studies*, 25 (1989), 43–67.

AUTHORIAL REVISION

In 1969 I received a letter from the curator of the Special Collections at the Boston University Library expressing interest in having my manuscripts. They would be preserved for researchers for all time under very scientific air–controlled conditions. *What* researchers? I am not overly modest, but that struck me as ludicrous. I remembered the humorist Robert Benchley's piece, "Why Does Nobody Collect Me?" I checked with a friend in the history department to see if it was a joke. He assured me they were serious. True, they were not so serious as to mention any money, but still, a compliment is a compliment. But I knew how I would respond, even if a fair sum had been dangled before me. I wasn't going to let anyone see my corrections, the tortuous road to the final printed version. While I had poked my professorial nose into other authors' revisions, my own were nobody's business.

It gets complicated when an author revises an already published version. Which version of Henry James's *The American* do you prefer? Consider the original description of the hero, Christopher Newman: "his eye was of a clear, cold grey, and save for a rather abundant moustache, he was clean shaved." (Why is grey the favorite color for men's eyes in American fiction of the 19th century? There's a subject for a dissertation.) What happened to Newman in the New York Edition, after James had freed himself from his own beard? "His eye was of a clear, cold grey, and save for the abundant droop of his moustache he spoke, as to cheek and chin, of the joy of the matutinal steel." Ah, "the matutinal steel"--is that metonymy? It is, unmistakably, late James.

I bought the 1976 *Collected Poems* of W.H. Auden, only to discover that, by the author's decree, "September 1, 1939" was missing. Does Auden have the right, after publishing it, to deprive us of one of the greatest and historically most important poems of the 20th century? According to Horace, what has once been published cannot be withdrawn. The editor, Edward Mendelson, acknowledges, "Some of Auden's readers have objected that his late revisions weaken the force of his early poems,

139

and that the original versions are always to be preferred." Before dropping "September 1, 1939" altogether, Auden ruined its most memorable line, "We must love one another or die." He changed to the merely biological cliché, "We must love one another and die." Julian Barnes recently speared that: "It's...about as interesting on the subject of the human condition, and as striking, as *We must listen to the radio and die* or *We must remember to defrost the fridge and die.*"

Readers have rights, and authors aren't necessarily the best judges of their own work. Virgil left orders, countermanded by the Emperor Augustus, that the *Aeneid* be destroyed as too imperfect. (The miniaturist Robert Herrick copied this attitude: "Julia, if I chance to die / Ere I print my Poetry; / I most humbly thee desire / To commit it to the fire: / Better 'twere my book were dead, / Than to live not perfected.") We'd have never shed tears over Little Nell if Dickens had had his way. It was his adviser John Forster who declared that it was necessary that she die. Some editions of *Great Expectations* print two endings: Bulwer Lytton proposed the happier one that brought Pip and Estella together after all. When James dramatized *The American,* instead of shutting up the lovely Claire de Cintré in a convent, he allowed Newman to marry her, as William Dean Howells and other readers had expected. It's disturbing to have vacillating authors, pulling rugs from under our feet.

Coleridge, characteristically, had trouble making up his mind about the second line in this stanza of "The Rime of the Ancient Mariner": "The fair breeze blew, the white foam flew, / The furrow followed free; / We were the first that ever burst / Into that silent sea." Having made a multitude of other changes between the 1798 and 1800 *Lyrical Ballads,* he printed in the 1817 *Sibylline Leaves* "The furrow stream'd off free," adding a note repudiating the earlier version: "I had not been long on board a ship before I perceived that this was the image as seen by a spectator from the shore, or from another vessel. From the ship itself the *Wake* appears like a brook flowing off from the stern." But in 1828 and subsequent editions the old line was restored. Apparently there is such a thing as being too precise.

That perfect poem, "Tithonus," did not spring whole out of Tennyson's head: "The woods decay, the woods decay and fall, / The vapours weep their burthen to the ground." It originally began hysterically: "Ay me! Ay me! The woods decay and fall, / The stars slope out and never rise again, / The vapours weep their substance to the ground." The final version opts for plosives over explosion.

Tone it down, whispered the Muse to William Blake also, at work on "The Tyger." Lower your voice. "Dare he laugh his work to see? / Dare he who made the lamb make thee?" No, better, "Did he smile his work to see? / Did he who made the Lamb make thee?" And drop that adjective, which is implicit in the noun: "Burnt in distant deeps or skies /

The cruel fire of thine eyes?" Make it, "In what distant deeps or skies / Burnt the fire of thine eyes?"

Speaking of fire and going from tigers to leopards, Emily Dickinson produced this Blake–like poem: "Blazing in Gold and quenching in Purple / Leaping like Leopards to the Sky / Then at the feet of the old Horizon / Laying her spotted face to die / Stooping as low as the Otter's Window / Touching the Roof and tinting the Barn / Kissing her Bonnet to the Meadow / And the Juggler of Day is gone." An alternate reading is, "Stooping as low as the kitchen window"; another, "as low as an oriel window." The modern editor Thomas H. Johnson observes, "One text is apparently as `final' as another. The reader may make the choice." That is easy, in my view: pick what Thomas Wentworth Higginson would eschew, Dickinson's patron and patroniser, who opposed the "odd" and insisted on "sensible" metaphors. His sun would set at man–made windows. And old Sol would be masculine.

As every eleventh–grader knows (or used to know), at the dedication of the burial ground at Gettysburg on November 19, 1863, a short speech was preceded by a long one. The golden–tongued former professor of Greek at Harvard, Edward Everett, held forth for two hours; Abraham Lincoln took less than three minutes. Less familiar are the differences between the President's first draft and his final version, which added thirty–three words for a total of 272. "...who here gave their lives that that nation might live. It is altogether fitting and proper that we should do this" had been: "who died here that the nation might live. This we may, in all propriety do." "Propriety" was too fancy and long and Latinate for the quintessential Lincoln. Amazingly the Gettysburg Address has 204 monosyllabic words, with only eighteen of three or more syllables.

To revert to another modest author, Shakespeare's text is slippery on account of his indifference, or downright hostility, to seeing his plays in print, which would spoil their novelty for playgoers. For authorial revision have been substituted the constructs and emendations of editors. The received text of *Hamlet* is an amalgam of Quarto 2 and First Folio. We ought to worry about this smoothed out and homogenized product, but we generally don't.

It takes the despised Quarto 1 to give us a jolt. "To be, or not to be, I there's the point." It would be pleasant to think that this is the bard himself caught struggling on the slopes, but it is more likely to be––with its "I" for "aye"––a copyist endeavoring to remember what he has heard, who lacks a written text. Still, this 1603 text, upon which so much scorn has been heaped, does offer us a Queen not guilty of straying during her first husband's lifetime, and, in the bedroom scene with her son (who, by the way, is staring at a Ghost ready for bed "in his night gowne") explicitly free of conspiracy: "But as I have a soule, I sweare by heaven, /

I never knew of this most horride murder." Maybe she doth protest too much, but it's something we want to hear from her.

Ben Jonson, careful craftsman, reminisced, "I remember the players have often mentioned it as an honor to Shakespeare, that in his writing (whatsoever he penned) he never blotted out a line. My answer hath been, `Would he had blotted a thousand!'" This is the slow writer envying the fast one. Milton, Jonson's heir as a classicist, also considered himself slow and did much blotting of which a record survives. Sir Henry Newton Puckering, a Royalist, in 1691 gave to Trinity College (Milton went to Christ's) Cambridge, nearly four thousand books and manuscripts, of which the greatest treasure went long uncatalogued and unnoticed: drafts in Milton's hand of "Lycidas" and "Comus" and other of his poems. Charles Lamb just didn't want to know about it. "I had thought of the `Lycidas' as of a full-grown beauty--as springing up with all its parts absolute--till, in an evil hour, I was shown the original copy of it, together with the other minor poems of the author, in the library of Trinity, kept like some treasure to be proud of. I wish they had thrown them in the Cam, or sent them after the latter Cantos of Spenser, into the Irish Channel. How it staggered me to see the fine things in their ore! interlined, corrected! as if their words were mortal, alterable, displaceable at pleasure! as if they might have been otherwise, and just as good! as if inspiration were made up of parts, and these fluctuating, successive, indifferent! I will never go into the workshop of any great artist again." Lamb has the Romantic shrinking from dry fruit, as signalled by his use of the punning phrase from the Fall, "in evil hour": "So saying, her rash hand in evil hour / Forth reaching to the fruit--" (*Paradise Lost*, IX, 780; Adam hurls it back at Eve, 1067).

Undergraduates are not usually made aware of the Cambridge (or Trinity) Manuscript. Who cares about textual variations? Who cares about poetry? Who cares about anything? It is a deadly syllogism. But maybe they're good for a romp, which "Lycidas" offers: "To sport with Amaryllis in the shade, / Or with the tangles of Neaera's hair." Those are not just allegorical figures--those are (to use an old-fashioned word) girls. In the latter instance, what are we doing, we playboys, playing with her hair? There is evidence that Milton was much preoccupied with hair, "the amorous net." (Locate the passages, including the Latin and Italian.) Is "with" possibly a spelling for *withe*, to twist? Will you believe that Milton originally wrote, instead of "Or with": "Hid in"! So we sport somehow with Amaryllis, while covered (*who* is covered?) with hair of another. Peekaboo.

In 1970 a Brooklyn College professor, in a letter to the London *Times Literary Supplement*, declared that the lines "never seemed to me to offer any difficulty of interpretation. The hair is pubic, is it not? At least it must be so on a second level of meaning which puts in its appearance here no less promptly than at the end of Canto IV of Pope's *Rape of the Lock*" (another revised poem).

The young poet, not being modern, toned down violence. The Elder Brother in *Comus* declares he will make the villain restore his sister, "Or drag him by the curls [hair again!] to a foul death, / Cursed as his life." What the poet first wrote was, "Or drag him by the curls and cleave his scalp / Down to the hips." That's a mighty cleave. "Scalp" was also dropped from "Lycidas": "gory scalp" became "gory visage."

The secular equivalent of a comparative edition of the three Synoptic Gospels is S.E. Sprott's 1973 *A Maske: The Earlier Versions*, which prints in parallel columns the Trinity College MS. of what the eighteenth century began calling *Comus*, the Bridgewater acting MS., and the first edition of 1637 (the year Jonson died). But the 1645 and the 1673 editions also have points of interest for any who appreciate that "God is in the details." Why was line 167, "Whom thrift keeps up about his Country gear," dropped in 1673? A lewd professor might say, because "gear" *can* mean "organs of generation" (*Oxford English Dictionary*, 5 b).

The MS. clarifies at least the original meaning of the Attendant Spirit's lofty scorn at the beginning of the *Maske* for earthlings who,

> with low-thoughted care
> strive to keepe up a fraile & feavourish beeing
> beyond the written date of mortall change
> confin'd & pester'd in this pinfold heere
> unmindful of the crowne that vertue gives

The "fraile & feavourish" ought to know when it is time to depart and stop struggling to linger on. It comes as a surprise that the prologue of a poem about chastity and virtue should stray onto a topic so much agonized over today: the prolongation of a life that may no longer be worth living. (The "pinfold" could be a hospital.) To quote from the Medical Directive published as a supplement to the Harvard Medical School Health Letter, June, 1990: "What kind of medical condition ['frail and feverish?'], if any, would make life hard enough that you would find attempts to prolong it undesirable? None? Intractable pain? Permanent dependence on others? Irreversible mental damage? Another condition you would regard as intolerable?" Echoing a key word of Milton's is a report in the journal *Science* (November, 1990) that we may be "trading off a longer life for a prolonged period of frailty and dependency." Adam after the fall reproaches death for "tardy execution" (*PL* X. 853) and Eve in her desperation urges, "Let us seek Death, or he not found, supply / With our own hands his office on ourselves" (X. 1001–02). But, as we might expect from his Christian belief, Milton is not on the side of Donne's defence of suicide *Bianthanatos*, or the Hemlock Society, however gloomy Michael's depiction of old age and its infirmities:

"This is old age; but then thou must outlive
Thy youth, thy strength, thy beauty, which will change
To withered weak and gray; thy senses then
Obtuse, all taste of pleasure must forgo
To what thou hast, and for the air of youth
Hopeful and cheerful, in thy blood will reign
A melancholy damp of cold and dry
To weigh thy spirits down, and last consume
The balm of life."   (XI. 538–46.)

As melancholy Jacques concluded, "sans teeth, sans eyes, sans taste, sans everything" (*As You Like It*, II. vii. 166). Adam accepts to bear "this cumbrous charge" that the Attendant Spirit had inveighed against, "till my appointed day ["the written date of mortall change"] / Of rend'ring up, and patiently attend / My dissolution." (XI. 549–52) The last five words were added in 1674, the last year of Milton's life. Patience was ever his message.

But we began with a red, or vanished herring. "Beyond the written date of mortall change" was deleted from the MS. and does not appear in the printed editions. We are left without its guidance to a passage that may have another meaning:

                              with low–thoughted care
Confined and pestered in this pinfold here,
Strive to keep up a frail and feverish being,
Unmindful of the crown that Virtue gives
After this mortal change, to her true servants
Amongst the enthroned gods on sainted seats.

A.S.P. Woodhouse in the Columbia *Variorum Commentary* finds "curiously inept" "Keightley's interpretation ('the love of life which is so strong in most men's bosoms') and Verity's elaboration (that men strive to live too long, instead of being glad when death releases them to a better life)." Woodhouse opts for "directing their cares and affections to material things, men strive in vain for life and being, attaining only an existence *frail* (transient: *OED* I b) and *Feaverish* (restless: *OED* 2)." The figurative has been preferred over the clinical. The upwardly mobile are really downwardly mobile. In the words of another 17th–century writer, "Their hot pursuit of pleasure, or constant drudgery in business, engages some men's thoughts elsewhere" (John Locke, An *Essay Concerning Human Understanding*, IV, Ch. 20, 6). It is a curious case of the author pointing first in one direction, and then––where? It is not necessarily a war of exclusives, as the intemperate get the health they deserve. In *De Doctrina Christiana* I. viii (Columbia *Works*, 15. 92) Milton lumps them with the suicides, since they "hasten death by vicious living" (*pravo victu accelerant*).

Is there a case where Milton *should have* revised but did not? His translation of "The Fifth Ode of Horace. Lib.I," "Rendered almost word for word," may end up one word too many in its last line: "To the stern God of Sea." Line–by–line commentary being hard to come by, I am aware of only three notes. The first dates from 1853 and issues from the Cambridge scholar the Reverend Arthur Macleane, in his edition of Horace for the *Bibliotheca Classica* series: "Milton translates 'the stern god of sea,' not observing that 'potens' governs 'maris' as 'potens Cypri,' C.i.3.1, and 'lyrae potens,' C.i.6.10."[1] In 1968 John Carey (of Oxford) made the same criticism, saying of "stern": "M.'s addition: Latin *potenti...maris deo*, to the god who is master of the sea."[2] To confirm that this is received doctrine, passed on from generation to generation, I can begin with my modest college textbook[3]––and then go on to weightier 19th– and 20th–century annotators, including Doering and Orelli (whom Macleane mentions in his Preface).[4] But in 1977 Robert Hodge, enough of a Latinist to have translated some of Milton's elegies, voiced no objection to Milton's construing, commenting only on his diction: "M changed 'powerful' (*potenti*) to 'stern,' to give the repudiation of oceanic sexuality a more sombre and definitive tone."[5] In 1986 Charles Martindale produced six pages on what he called, after Dryden, Milton's "metaphrase" that were blithely free of the entanglements of previous commentary.[6]

In this small, delicate issue of construction, if there is one reputable authority on the side of Milton we cannot pronounce Milton wrong. Davis P. Harding, who also does not mention the problem, happens to provide such support by quoting a prose translation by the preeminent John W. Mackail which concludes: "to the mighty God of the Sea,"[7] On the other hand, the Loeb Library translator, C.E. Bennett, has (like Carey after him): "to the god who is master of the sea."[8]

The latter interpretation is based (as we can see from Macleane) on a study of similar instances in Horace. "Horace is extremely fond of adjectives with the gen."[9] But Acron, or whoever wrote the scholia attributed to him, did not so read our poem.[10] And only forty–two years after Milton's version first appeared it was reprinted in *Odes and Satyrs of Horace that have been done into English by the Most Eminent Hands*, with Philip Horneck's version that has "the Great Ruler of the Sea."[11] This 1715 collection is the predecessor to Sir Ronald Storrs' 1959 *Ad Pyrrham: A Polyglot Collection of Translations*.[12] Almost invariably in the early versifiers gathered by Storrs we find "potenti" treated as a descriptive adjective: "mighty" (William Browne), "powerful" (Dr. "Barton"––for Barten––Holyday), "potent" (Henry Rider), "great" (Sir Richard Fanshawe). As we move forward in time the contest is between "mighty" (William Boscawen, Leigh Hunt, Francis B.T. Coutts-Nevill) and "great" (John Nott, Eugene Liés, Bishop Christopher Storrs, "b. 1889"). Two

Germans have "mächtigen." The 15th-century P. Pavolo Gualterio Aretino has "del gran Nettuno." The French can have it both ways: "Qu'au Dieu puissant de la marine" (Luc de la Porte, 1584).

Without ransacking libraries for a poll of some two hundred English versions of *Ad Pyrrham,* the above is a start at showing that a goodly number of worthies, of several centuries, are in accord with Milton's treatment of *potenti.*

The Miltonist should go on to consider a parallel case in his own author. Around 1647, as he began writing his *History of Britain,* Milton had occasion to produce a blank verse translation from the Latin:

> Consultation had, *Brutus* taking with him *Gerion* his Diviner, and twelv of the ancientest, with wonted Ceremonies before the inward shrine of the Goddess, in Verse, as it seems the manner was, utters his request, *Diva potens nemorum* &c.[13]

The Latin verses came from Commelin's *Rerum Britannicarum.*[14] Oddly enough, the first three words are reminiscent of the first line of Horace's *Carmen Saeculare*: "Phoebe silvarumque potens Diana." How did Milton handle the "potens" construction this time? Did he say, "Stern goddess of the groves"? No; he wrote: "Goddess of Shades."

What this change signifies I am not sure. Any who date the Horace translation (added to the 1673 poems) early, making it a schoolboy exercise, and who side with Macleane and Carey, can argue the author has learned more Latin. This conclusion is, however, weakened by the extraordinary freedom with which Commelin's first line is treated, words being passed over that a "word for word" version should have had. "Goddess of Shades, and Huntress, who at will" is not adequate to "Diva potens nemorum, terror silvestribus apris." Anyone who condenses "terror to the boars of the woods" to "Huntress" might well omit an adjective for the goddess.

Before settling on "A thing of beauty is a joy forever," Keats wrote, "A thing of beauty is a constant joy." No, emends the literary scholar, A thing of beauty is a wavering joy, as we have seen.

Another puzzle, in these days of rushing into print we cannot fathom a Shakespeare who never published his plays, the greatest writer of all indifferent to fame, and taking early and obscure retirement to Stratford. It remained for the second greatest to call his predecessor "great heir of Fame" in his own first publication, contributed to the 1632 Second Folio. Milton was to write endlessly about fame but was very slow to claim it. His couplets on Shakespeare were unsigned. The *Maske* was printed in 1637 because Henry Lawes the composer got tired of copying it "to give my several friends satisfaction." The author was not named. In 1638 "Lycidas" appeared, proclaiming (line 70), "Fame is the spur that the clear spirit doth raise"--and bore only the initials J.M. Thus,

John Crowe Ransom headed a famous essay, "A Poem Nearly Anonymous." Totally anonymous was Milton's debut in English prose, *Of Reformation Touching Church Discipline in England: and the Causes that hitherto have hindered it,* 1641. His second and third tracts were also anonymous. *Of Education* was anonymous: it did not even have a title page. He waited dangerously long to put out *Paradise Lost,* "long choosing, and beginning late," after going blind working for the regicides, experiencing poor health in his fifties, and narrowly escaping with his life at the revengeful Restoration. Of such patient stuff--and risk-taking-- was his greatness made. "They also serve who only stand and wait" (who does any waiting these days?)--has its real life counterpart in a little- known description, by a German emissary, Hermann Mylius, of Milton, the Latin secretary, *standing and waiting* for orders at a meeting of the Lords Commissioners in Whitehall in October 1651. The grandees and other officers are seated at a long table. There is even an empty chair, but Milton, unknown and of no interest to them as a poet, is not invited to occupy it. He stands very attentive ("sehr attent sich bezeiget"). A man too proud to let it be known how little he sees (within half a year he will be totally blind) peers intently, his hearing making up for his handicap, as in the highly aural *Paradise Lost.* This is a far cry from the frontispiece to W. Melville Harris's 1923 biography, which shows Milton seated at a writing table, with Oliver Cromwell in full military gear standing alongside. Unfortunately there is no evidence that Milton and Cromwell were ever even in the same room together.

NOTES

1. Macleane, ed., *Opera Omnia*, 4th ed. revised by George Long (London: Whittaker and Bell, 1881), 21.
2. Carey, ed., with Alastair Fowler, *The Poems of John Milton* (London: Longmans, 1968), 97.
3. "16. *maris*: depends upon *potenti* (who rules)." John W. Basore and Shirley H. Weber, eds., *A Book of Latin Poetry* (Boston: Allyn and Bacon, 1925), 213.
4. Cf. ad loc. Fredericus G. Doering (Oxford, 1838); I. Gaspar Orellius 4th ed. (Berlin, 1886); E.C. Wickham (Oxford, 1896); T.E. Page, A. Palmer, A.S. Wilkins (London, 1896); Clement L. Smith (New York, 1904); H. Darnley Naylor (Cambridge, 1922); R.G.M. Nisbit and Margaret Hubbard (Oxford, 1970).
5. John Broadbent and Hodge, eds., *Samson Agonistes, Sonnets, & c.* (Cambridge: Cambridge University Press, 1977), 20. Charles Lamb, who in *The Last Essays of Elia* commences "Amicus Redivivus" with a quotation from "Lycidas", is pleased to have the following echo towards the end: "At their head Arion––or is it G.D.?––in his singing garments marcheth singly, with harp in hand, and votive garland, which Machaon (or Dr. Hawes) snatcheth straight, intending to suspend it to the stern God of Sea." *Complete Works and Letters* (New York: Modern Library, 1935), 189.
6. Martindale, *John Milton and the Transformation of Ancient Epic* (Totowa, N.J.: Barnes & Noble), 42–47.
7. Harding, *The Club of Hercules* (Urbana: University of Illinois Press, 1962), 129, n. 25, quoting Mackail's *Studies in Humanism* (London, 1938), 68.
8. Bennett, ed., *Odes and Epodes* (Cambridge: Harvard University Press, 1914, 1946), 19.
9. Page, Palmer, Wilkins, 207.
10. Only relevant note reads: "MARIS DEO: NEPTUNO." Otto Keller, ed., *Pseudacronis Scholia in Horatium Vetustiora* (Stuttgart: Teubner, 1967).
11. (London, 1715), 14.
12. Oxford: Oxford University Press.
13. *Complete Prose Works of John Milton*, Vol. 5, Part I, *The History of Britain*, ed., French Fogle (New Haven: Yale University Press, 1971), 14.
14. *Ibid.*, n. 39.

For Product Safety Concerns and Information please contact our EU
representative GPSR@taylorandfrancis.com
Taylor & Francis Verlag GmbH, Kaufingerstraße 24, 80331 München, Germany